Islam, Isra

the Church

Islam, Israel and the Church

Marcel Rebiai

Sovereign World

Sovereign World Ltd
PO Box 784
Ellel
Lancaster LA1 9DA
England

www.sovereignworld.com
www.facebook.com/sovereignworld

Originally published in 2004 under the title *Islam, Israel und die Gemeinde, Der Kampf um die Erwählung* by Schleife Verlag, Switzerland, ISBN 3–907827–42–2. All rights reserved.

Translated from German into English by Susan Wiesmann

Quotations from the Koran were translated into English from the authoritative German translation by Rudi Paret, fourth edition 1985, Kohlhammer Publishers, Germany. The sura numbers differ in some standard translations.

ISBN 978-185240-730-8

The publishers aim to produce books which will help to extend and build up the Kingdom of God. We do not necessarily agree with every view expressed by the authors, or with every interpretation of Scripture expressed. We expect readers to make their own judgment in the light of their understanding of God's Word and in an attitude of Christian love and fellowship.

Typeset by CRB Associates, Reepham, Norfolk

Contents

Introduction

As the author of this book, I am part of a Christian community, the *Community of Reconciliation*, which has followed the Messiah's calling to be ambassadors of reconciliation (see 2 Corinthians 5:20). Our community of families and single people has for years shared our everyday lives with Jews, with Islamic and Christian Arabs, with Israelis and Palestinians.

In the midst of increasing aggression, violence and counter-violence, the daily lives of our Jewish and Arab friends are colored by fear, helplessness, hopelessness, accusations, bitterness and hatred – with no sign of a genuine way out.

Through our personal relationships with both Jews and Arabs we attempt to bring them friendship, acceptance and the hope of the Gospel while giving practical help with social needs. We bring the message that peace and reconciliation are first of all a question of the heart.

As we live in friendship on the Jewish as well as the Arab side, we want to be a bridge of reconciliation by bringing the hope of the Gospel in word and deed into the lives of our friends. We enable and encourage reconciliation and peace on an individual plane as well as between families and groups.

Through the trust which both Jewish and Arab friends have gained in our team, many attitudes toward the Arab and Jewish "enemy" have been changed. Through their efforts towards friendships on both sides, our members build a bridge which makes it possible for the contentious and estranged to find new paths to each other within a framework of trust.

Standing between the two fronts is incredibly demanding. No matter how close we are to others, sympathetically bearing their pain and burdens, we must refuse to be emotionally drawn into their hostile prejudices. This requires much discipline and intentional living, which I believe is possible only in the power of God.

We are totally on the side of the God of the Bible, including his promises and plans for the Jewish people Israel, as well as his promises and plans for the Arab people (Isaiah 19:22–23). Because we know that the God of Israel desires to be the God of the Arab people as well, we can have big hearts of love and dedication both for Jews and for Arabs.

We are in contact with many Palestinian families; we offer them practical social aid, and help them bring up their children. We bring administrative, legal, and spiritual help to men and women in prison. Over and over again we testify to them about hope and reconciliation.

On the Jewish side, our team also shares in many lives, bringing support, help and comfort; we declare that there is hope because Israel's God lives and cares for his people. He intends to reveal himself anew to his people in the countenance of the Messiah and king of the Jews, *Yeshua* (Jesus) of Nazareth.

This book is not a comprehensive academic treatment, but rather a summary of various lectures and articles on the topics of Islam, Israel and Christianity. The intent is to shed light from various angles, to inform and to stimulate discussion.

Marcel Rebiai

Chapter 1

Focus on Islam

After the terror attacks of September 11, 2001, in New York, I have the impression that broad sectors of the public see two primary sources of evil in the present world: not Islam, as one would naturally expect as a result of the attacks, but Israel and believing Christians. Both are often given the stigmatizing label "fundamentalists." Both supposedly endanger world security and peaceful co-existence.

How do I reach this surprising conclusion?

Islam – a "religion of peace"?

It has been proven that the 9/11 attacks, which ruthlessly violated all principles for handling international conflicts, were perpetrated by convinced Muslims. These are persons who are absolutely serious about their faith and their religion. They base their lives exclusively on their religious sources, that is, the Koran and the *hadith* (traditional teaching on the life and thoughts of Mohammed and his followers).

However, the thoughts and actions of the terrorists can scarcely be comprehended or accepted by a non-Muslim, especially one from Western culture. Many politicians and religious leaders, in alliance with the media and the Islamic intelligentsia, are trying to make us believe that the attack had nothing to do with true Islam. They promote the view that these terrorists were not genuine Muslims but the kind of fanatics that can be found in every religion and culture.

In their desire for a conflict-free and tolerant world, many are quick to claim that Islam is a religion of peace which rejects violence against those with other beliefs. Nevertheless, the fact is that Islamic states such as Saudi Arabia, Pakistan, Sudan, Afghanistan, and Iran forbid every form of public expression or practice of non-Islamic religion. They pursue missionaries with criminal laws and punish conversion to the Christian faith by death, on the basis of *sharia* (religious law).

Many in Western society seem either unaware of this or consider it an insignificant expression of Islam's violent nature. Indignation over human rights violations tends to be for the Israeli-Palestinian conflict. An example of this is the Geneva conference on Israeli human rights violations against the Palestinian people.

Equating Christianity and Islam

In an effort to avoid casting any suspicion or doubt on Islam, we are reminded of terrorism in the name of the Christian religion. The Catholic–Protestant conflicts, the Inquisition and the Crusades are cited to draw attention to the confusion and aberrations in all religions. Christianity and Islam are seen as religions which are equally easy to abuse.

It is true that Christianity has often been and still is mis-used for political and personal gain. But whoever equates Islam and Christianity has understood neither the one nor the other.

Islam as partner?

In order to win over Islamic nations as partners in the battle against terrorism, leading Western nations reassure them that they do not question their religion, but respect and protect it. As far as I know, Islam is the only religion which the UN human rights conference in Durban protected. They accomplished this with a resolution against "Islamophobia" (pathological fear of Islam).

In the Western world it is considered improper to express criticism of Islam. Whoever does so may be suspected of intolerance, prejudice, or even racism. And what does the liberal post-modern person fear more than such a label? The Islamic intelligentsia and spiritual leadership are aware of these fears and play the tolerance cards brilliantly. They demand rights for Islam which Islam would never accord other religious groups.

No religious freedom in Islamic states

Where can churches or synagogues, Christian or Jewish schools now be built in countries such as Saudi Arabia, Iran, or Pakistan – who are all being wooed for the anti-terror coalition?

The Islamic countries have a clear stance, claiming that whatever they do or don't do at home is their own business. Their world-view, lifestyle, and culture, which a non-Muslim cannot understand, must be accepted and respected. A conference of Islamic secretaries of state several years ago concluded that enforcing a Western definition of human rights amounts to intellectual colonialism and paternalism.

Amar Moussa, former Egyptian secretary of state and now president of the Arab League, recently warned Western nations against a confrontation between civilizations. He demanded that they eliminate every form of enmity, rejection, and suppression of the Islamic world. Terrorism should be understood as the result of oppression and poverty. Once these were eliminated, he maintained, nothing would hinder worldwide peace.

Significantly, it would seem that Amar Moussa can be confident of the Western world's agreement. Many are quick to conclude that it is the radical elements which are the sole problem in every religion. Therefore the conflict-producing extremists, the peace-hinderers, and the seats of unrest must be neutralized. The Islamic nations leave no doubt about who they believe fulfills these criteria: confessing Christians and Israel.

Confessing Christians: the disturbing factor

Why Christians? Christians are convinced that those who live in the Islamic world, like all others, have the right to hear the good news of Jesus Christ. They consider it their duty to make the Gospel available for Muslims' consideration. This attitude leads to confrontation with Islamic governments and religious leaders.

The question is, is it right for Western church leaders, politicians, and media to oppose missionaries and forbid their work among Islamic peoples in order to meet Islam's demand for unconditional acceptance? Must the West sacrifice central tenets of the Gospel, along with the confessing Christians themselves, in order to avoid conflicts with Islam? Is this the only way to reduce Islamic aggression, violence, and terror so the West can protect its own interests and security?

Controversy over Israel

It appears that the Western world is increasingly willing to sacrifice Israel, as well, in order to ensure its own security, which is threatened by the Islamic world's unpredictability. As the Durban conference showed, all Islamic states – not only the Palestinian representatives – are united in their enmity toward Israel. Their co-operation in the USA's anti-terror coalition is made contingent on the West's attitude toward Israel.

Countries like Iran and Syria, which until now have been proscribed because they were considered shelters for various terror cells, are suddenly being wooed by the West. At the same time Israel is informed that its participation in the coalition would aggravate too many countries, especially Islamic ones.

Syria is even allowed to be a member of the UN's permanent Security Council without protest from the US, let alone from the EU – despite being well-known for supporting terror organizations such as Hisbollah and having occupied parts of Lebanon for years. The only ones who were criticized for their position on Lebanon were the Israelis, prior to their withdrawal in May 2000.

Two definitions of terror

Surprisingly, even President Bush has begun speaking of a Palestinian state. He appears to have two definitions of terror. Terror which affects his country is to be fought with all means. But Israel's daily experiences – murderous ambushes against buses, cars, restaurants, and pedestrians – is not terror in the same sense.

Israel is under increasing pressure to bow to Islam's demands by withdrawing to a minimum of territory and giving up holy cities such as Jerusalem and Hebron. Otherwise Israel's "provocation" of the Islamic world would endanger Western interests. It will soon be seen how much substance Tony Blair's, George W. Bush's, Gerhard Schroeder's, and other

Western politicians' present assertions of friendship for Israel will be retained.

House of peace, house of war

One cannot make alliances with and promises to Islam thinking this can all be reinterpreted later. Using force to secure one's right is not just the bad habit of a few naughty Islamic boys. It has to do with the very character of Islam.

The word *Islam* means not only peace, but also submission. In Muslim thought, the world is divided into the *house of Islam* (house of peace) and the *house of war* (every non-Islamic territory). There is peace only for those who have been transferred from the house of war to the house of Islam through subjection.

It would be a good thing for Western church leaders, politicians, and media personnel to seriously study the basic principles of Islam. They should dare an attempt to understand these from the standpoint of Islamic thinking rather than from Western humanistic presuppositions. Otherwise, the West's naïveté about Islamic self-understanding could lead to a rude awakening.

The message of love

We disciples of Jesus clearly distinguish between Islam as a religion or ideology and the Muslims as persons. Muslims are – just like all of us – persons who are loved by God. Jesus gave his life for them in order to open the way to the Father's house. We love, esteem, and respect them, at the same time distancing ourselves from the religion which influences, drives, and imprisons them.

It is challenging to take a stand regarding Islam. But if we really believe that people can experience salvation and peace solely through the name of Jesus, the Messiah, it is unloving and irresponsible to ignore Muslims. This is what happens when we display tolerance and indifference and withhold the good news of the Gospel from them.

I hope with all my heart that we have the courage not to bow when we are questioned and threatened. We must acquire our own conviction on the basis of God's Word. Such conviction will make us a sign of hope and a light in the darkness – in our relationship to Israel as well as in our love toward the Islamic peoples.

Chapter 2

Islam and Its Relationship to Israel and the Christian Community

On the basis of fifteen years' study of Islam, I wish to illuminate the essence and rationale, the beliefs and the spiritual background of Islam, especially its relationship to Jews and Christians.

It would fill whole libraries of books to present the complete scope of Islam's character and self-understanding, to say nothing of its controversy with the Jewish people and the Christian faith. The differences between folk religion, tradition, orthodoxy, practical rites, mysticism, and reform movements of various Islamic branches are a broad subject. The different Islamic cultures from Indonesia to Afghanistan to Morocco also demonstrate that Islam appears in thousands of forms in everyday life.

Nevertheless we can speak of *the* Islamic religion, for in the Islamic world there is an identity which unifies all the differences. This identity is the foundation of Islam, a self-understanding common to all Muslims, in which they stand together against the non-Islamic world. We will now illuminate this basis of Islam in order to shed more light on the increasingly intensive conflict with Israel and with the Christian world.

In my presentation of Islam and its relationship to Israel and the Christian Church I make no claim to an exhaustive treatment or to so-called objectivity. On the one hand it is obviously not simple to make an exhaustive portrayal of Islam. On the other hand, I also believe that God alone is objective. No person judges without a value system.

Whatever people present or describe is a product of their world-view, of their faith or lack of faith, of their thinking, morals and values. I myself think and judge as one for whom the message of the Bible is the highest authority and the binding truth for all mankind.

Since September 11, 2001, it is increasingly necessary to understand Islam in its relationship to the Christian and the Jewish world. It is being said everywhere that Islam is a peaceful religion which is very similar to Christianity and Judaism, since it is monotheistic. But does this correspond with the facts?

The idea that Islam has a common basis to Jewish and Christian thought seems to me the wishful thinking of the world and of some Muslims who have adapted to Western culture. The idea is to soothe those in the West who, frightened by Islamic terror, are searching for something secure to grasp.

But this is not the thinking of Muhammad, the central figure of Islam. Let us look at his own words! In the Koran, sura 109:15 he said, *"You unbelievers* [by which he meant Jews and Christians], *I do not honor what you honor, I do not serve what you serve, and you do not honor what I honor . . . You have your religion and I have mine."*

Before looking more closely at Islam, I will briefly sketch the three so-called monotheistic religions.

Judaism

Judaism is concerned with a certain nation, with a people bound to a specific land. Jews consider themselves a people called and chosen by God, under God's rule in the land he gave them. This causes Judaism to be a testimony for all peoples that the God of Israel is the sole true, living God, who is the God of the nations. The Jewish people's relationship to God, living under his rule, makes it a light to the heathen who do not know the God of Israel.

Thus we read in Isaiah 43:10,

> *"You are my witnesses," declares the* LORD,
>   *"and my servant whom I have chosen,*
> *so that you* [and the nations] *may know and believe me*
>   *and understand that I am he.*
> *Before me no god was formed,*
>   *nor will there be one after me."*
>
> (see also Isaiah 45:21 and 44:8)

Judaism knows neither missions (i.e. winning adherents) nor territorial expansion. It gathers a people under the reign of the God of Israel in the land God has promised them. We could call Judaism a national religion.

Christianity

The first disciples of Christ were Jews. Christianity not only grew out of biblical Judaism, but it is still based on the Old Testament, the Jewish Bible. Christians recognize that Jesus is the Messiah who was awaited by the Jewish people. According to the prophet Isaiah (chapter 53), this Messiah must come to remove his people's guilt through his sacrificial death and to fulfill his promises to the Jewish people, and through them, to all peoples.

In Jeremiah 31 we read,

> " 'The time is coming,' declares the LORD,
>   'when I will make a new covenant
> with the house of Israel . . .
> This is the covenant I will make . . .
>   after that time . . .
> I will put my law in their minds
>   and write it on their hearts . . . ' "
>
> (Jeremiah 31:31, 33)

The time of salvation and the restoration of God's kingdom has come in the Messiah Jesus, as written in John 3:16,

> "For God so loved the world that he gave his one and only Son, that whoever believes in him shall not perish but have eternal life."

The Gospel is the restoration of God's reign in the hearts of individuals. It is a universal message to the individual regarding his relationship to God and to his neighbor.

The worldwide Christian Church is neither an ethnic nor a national entity. It is a fellowship of persons who together confess that they have received forgiveness of sins through the Messiah Jesus and now participate in God's kingdom.

Differences in race, peoples, and nations, between class and gender are relatively insignificant. Only our relationship with God through the Messiah, and with our neighbor, is important.

Islam

Islam does not comprise a certain people, even though historically speaking it began among Arabs and the Arab world still claims leadership within Islam. Nor is it concerned with a particular land, although Islamic holy places such as Mecca and Medina exist, places upon which only Muslims may tread.

Islam does not strive for the conversion of individuals. It is unable to comprehend salvation as presented in the Gospel. From an Islamic point of view, it is not only unreasonable, but indeed blasphemous that Allah himself would identify with the guilt of his creatures and suffer in their stead in order to redeem them.

Allah is so endlessly lofty, so omnipotent, so majestic, that he cannot be thought of in any direct relationship to his creation, except that it honors him through obedience to his law. Allah knows that man is by nature weak, with a tendency to evil.

According to the Koran, from the beginning Allah himself created man with the capacity to sin as well as to fear him. He challenged man to overcome sin through obedience to his law, in order to achieve what is good (sura 91:7, 8). By keeping the commands and rules of Islam, man himself is able to live a life pleasing to Allah. There is no need for salvation, for each one can produce his own happiness – that is, if Allah wills it.

The center of Islam is Allah's law, to which all creation must submit, so that God may be honored through the keeping of his laws. There is no liberation of a people from slavery, like Israel's exodus from Egypt; there is no redemption from darkness and insurmountable original sin, as in Christianity.

One is not led into a personal loving relationship with Allah, nor is there any redemption history which restores a broken relationship between Allah and man. There is only submission to the law as Allah revealed it through Muhammad in the Koran.

Islam, the sole true religion

Non-Muslims think of Islam as a world religion alongside Judaism and Christianity, one which was founded by Muhammad in the seventh century. For Muslims, however, this is a devaluation of Islam because for them Islam is simply *the* religion.

In sura 3:19 we read, *"The only true religion before God is Islam."* And in sura 30:30, *"So set thou thy face steadily and truly to the Faith: God's handiwork according to the pattern on which He has made mankind. That is the standard Religion, but most among mankind understand not."*

For Muslims, Islam is not the religion of men who have a certain mutual faith and a mutual cultural and religious identity. They see it as the sole possible attitude toward Allah: *submitting* to his will, *obeying* his commands, and *surrendering* all areas of life to his law. Thus a Muslim is a person who has unreservedly submitted himself to Allah's will and command. Islam is a faith, a way of life, and a movement to establish Allah's will, laws, and ordinances in the whole world.

Adam, the "first Muslim"

For Muslims, Islam did not begin with Muhammad's appearance in Mecca, in AD 610, or with the beginning of the Islamic calendar in 622, the year of his flight (*hijra*) from Mecca to Medina, as non-Muslims see it historically. For Muslims, Islam began with man's creation and his appointment as Allah's representative on earth.

Sura 2:30ff., *"Behold, thy Lord said to the angels, 'I will create a vice-regent on earth . . .' "*; v. 34, *"And behold, we said to the angels, 'Bow down to Adam,' and they bowed down"*; v. 37, *"Then learnt Adam from his Lord words. Here Adam already called himself Muslim."* Sura 7:172, *"God said . . . 'Am I not your lord?' They said, 'Yes, we do thus testify!' "*

Adam thus demonstrated that Islam is the sole natural religion of man. Muhammad's message brought the final form of Islam, which is binding for all humanity. The Koran portrays his revelation as the word of God. In the Sunna and Hadith,

Muhammad's way of life, habits and thoughts are passed down as the binding example and standard for all Muslims.

According to Islam, Muhammad's message not only revealed the heathens' godlessness and darkness, but also corrected the aberration and perversion of those with Scriptures, primarily Jews and Christians. All are called to man's natural state, Islam, so that Allah does not destroy them.

Submission to Islam

For the heathen there could only be two possibilities: submission (surrender) to Islam's reign, or death. Sura 9:5, *"But when the forbidden months are past, then fight the pagans ... seize them, beleaguer them, and lie in wait for them ... but if they repent ... then open the way for them; for God is oft-forgiving, most merciful ... "*

Ultimately that applies to Jews and Christians also. The only true believer could be one who believed Muhammad's message and acknowledged Islam's reign over his life. Sura 5:77ff.: *"O people of the Book, exceed not the bounds of your faith ... If only they had believed in God, in the Apostle, and in what hath been revealed to him ... Strongest among men in enmity to the believers wilt thou find the Jews and pagans ... "*

But for the unbelievers – Jews as well as Christians – submission to Islam is required. If they remain beyond the pale of Islamic law, they should receive hard, merciless treatment in this life; and in the hereafter, judgment and hell.

Sura 9:29–30, *"Fight those who believe not in Allah nor the Last Day ... nor acknowledge the religion of truth, fight them until they pay the tribute with willing submission ... The Jews call Ezra a son of God, and the Christians call Christ the son of God; in this they but imitate what the unbelievers of old used to say. God's curse be on them; how they are deluded away from the Truth!"*

Muhammad as a Messiah figure

Since Islam is man's natural religion, a non-Muslim's condition is unnatural, i.e. perverted, and thus an abomination to Allah. Beyond the so-called *shirk* (bringing someone or something on an equal footing with Allah), the worst sin is that of pulling a Muslim away from Islam. This is worse than even murder or deception.

In sura 2:214 it is written, *"Leading astray from Allah's way and denying the holy mosque and driving his people from it is worse in Allah's sight; leading astray is worse than murder."*

In all four Islamic law schools, both defection from Islam and wooing someone away from Islam are punishable by death. Leaving or questioning Islam insults the majesty of Allah, to which the only response can be death. Since Muhammad proclaimed Allah's will, everyone who questions him must be put to death. Sura 4:82, *"Who obeys Muhammad obeys God and who insults Muhammad insults God."*

Muhammad represents Allah on earth; he is Allah's deputy. He is prophet, ruler, and imam (prayer leader in the mosque). As prophet he reveals Allah's will; as ruler he subjects the world to Allah's will and enforces God's commands; and as imam he intercedes before Allah for Muslims, who can be saved from judgment solely through his intercession.

As prophet, king, and priest, Muhammad embodies all the characteristics of the Messiah. Islam calls him the essence of all divine prophecies, the "seal of the prophets." As the Messiah figure, he is thus superior to everyone before him, including Abraham, Moses, and Jesus. Therefore he ultimately has a divine claim to obedience, in spite of all Islamic assertions to the contrary that he is only a human and himself needs Allah's forgiveness. Sura 4:80, *"Who obeys Muhammad obeys God."*

As the essence of what is pleasing to Allah, Muhammad is not just the central figure of Islam, but its very center. He exemplifies for all men what a Muslim should be, according to Allah. Since Allah in his eminence and majesty is so unapproachable for normal men that we can speak of an absent god, the Muslim is primarily and continually confronted with the thoughts and acts of Muhammad.

Islam as an anthropocentric religion

Islam, which prides itself on being an absolutely monotheistic religion, is in its essence actually anthropocentric, i.e. man is in the center. The intellect, the humanly possible, the given needs, desires, and limits of man determine the measure of a Muslim's actions and beliefs.

A large part of the so-called revelations in the Koran serve to explain Muhammad's life and actions, to justify and protect him especially where he claimed other rights than normal Muslims. Thus he was allowed to have not merely four but nine wives, as well as his concubines and women slaves. He had the right to demand that his adopted son get divorced because Muhammad desired this son's wife. He could attack and fight his enemies, mainly Jews in Medina, during what were generally considered war-free, peaceful times – holy months which had previously been respected by all the tribes, by Jews and Arabs. He commissioned or condoned his enemies' assassination.

As Allah's representative, Muhammad was spared from all judgment and accountability, and was above every moral code, custom, or ethnic consideration. In order to set up the reign of Islam, Allah allowed him every means, including trickery and deception, from breach of contract to murder. It is said, after all, that pulling a person away from true Islamic faith is far worse than killing.

These are not just insinuations. The Koran itself and the traditions speak clearly regarding Muhammad's character and conduct.

The beginnings of Islam

Why did Islam never acknowledge that it is a post-Christian religion, even though historically speaking it began at least 2,000 years after Judaism and 600 after Christianity? Why did Islam, in spite of its (obviously distorted) use of the Old and New Testaments, never admit that it was inspired by or at least arose from them?

On the contrary, Islam considers the Old and New Testaments originally Islamic revelation which was falsified by man. The coming of Muhammad was even supposedly prophesied there, e.g. in John's Gospel.

In order to understand this, as well as Islam's present relationship to Jews and Christians, we must look at Islam's origins. I do this without claiming to be totally comprehensive.

Muhammad realized that his people's religious rites and customs were less a matter of religion than expedience. In pre-Islamic time, the Kaaba in Mecca was a central holy place to which Arab tribes made pilgrimages. There, through religious rites, they attempted to secure for themselves luck and success in business and life.

Arab religious culture of the time was a mixture of polytheism, animism, and fetishism. Even then the Kaaba was thought to be the dwelling of a god. It was a principal idol. Not only religious life, but society itself was rapidly disintegrating. Murdering girls was a daily occurrence; alcohol and gambling brought many to ruin.

Muhammad was concerned about his people's future. As the son of a poor side branch of the suppressed Quraish clan, he initially had no influence whatsoever. But because he was a skilled businessman, a very wealthy and influential woman fifteen years his senior, named Kadisha, married him and he carried out business for her.

During his business trips to Christian Byzantium he came in

contact with Jews and with Christian monks. From them Muhammad learned about the existence of the one God, Creator of heaven and earth, who had revealed himself to Jews and Christians and given them holy Scriptures. He was impressed by the piety of the monks, who often lived in desert caves.

In addition, in Mecca he met many of the heretics whom the Byzantine Church had banished to the Arabian Desert. From them he gained a false understanding of the Trinity, consisting of Father, Son, and Maria. This found its way into the Koran.

How Muhammad became a prophet

Muhammad was inspired and fascinated by the idea of a mighty God. Even in pre-Islamic times there was the concept of one God above all the various gods and idols, so to speak a father-god. This was later called *"the* God," *al-illah,* from which the word *Allah* derived.

Muhammad withdrew increasingly from his business, with the desire to receive a message for his people. He apparently had such drastic religious encounters and experiences that he himself later said he had wanted to take his own life. They were so fearsome that he no longer wanted to expose himself to them. He was not sure whether he had encountered demons.

However, his wife and a so-called Christian relative encouraged him to continue these religious encounters in order to become a prophet to his people. Therefore Muhammad began proclaiming the messages which he claimed to have received from the angel Gabriel.

At first Muhammad's message was very simple and oriented itself primarily according to Jewish-Christian teaching. When the inhabitants of Mecca turned against him because of his campaign against the myriads of idols, demanding proof that his message was of divine origin, he referred to Jews and Christians as his witnesses. He was convinced that he proclaimed exactly the same message they did, even though he had never read the Bible, for he was illiterate.

Muhammad considered the Jews his chief witnesses. The Christians confused him too much with their doctrine of the Trinity, in spite of their positive attitude toward him. He still had the impression that they believed in three gods, namely God the Father, Son, and Maria, God's mother.

During Muhammad's controversy with the Meccans, who rejected him, Arabs from the neighboring city of Medina were impressed by his preaching. They immediately called him to Medina to help them. Blood vengeance between Arabs and Jews there was threatening to wipe out whole tribes and destroy the community.

In 622, which is known as the year of the *Hijra*, Muhammad and his followers moved to Medina, where Arabs and around 40,000 Jews lived alongside each other in large clans. With his authority and charisma, Muhammad's successful mediation stopped the blood feuding. He proved to be a capable statesman by giving the city a law regulating relationships.

As a result, the first Islamic community was born in Medina. Muhammad was both prophet and ruler.

Muhammad is rejected

After thus establishing himself, Muhammad turned to the Jews, assuming they would accept and confirm him as prophet. This would have led the Arabs to acknowledge his divine revelations.

But the Jews made unmistakably clear to him that they were waiting for one prophet only, namely Elijah, who would proclaim the coming of the Messiah. They said Muhammad had absolutely nothing in common with Elijah. He was even derided by some Jewish poets.

This encounter with the Medina Jews was a great disappointment for Muhammad and a serious blow to his sense of authority and self-esteem. The Jews there told him that rather than God having revealed himself, Muhammad was listening to demonic whisperings. Of all people, his crown witnesses rejected him!

The meaning of Jerusalem

Because Muhammad at first believed he had received the same revelation as the Jews and was one of their prophets, he and his followers prayed toward Jerusalem, like the Jews. He believed it was the city of the prophets and the center of divine revelation, even after he was alienated from the Jews.

In the interpretation of sura 17 in the Koran it is said that one night Muhammad had to ride to Jerusalem on his winged horse Alburak in order to ascend to heaven from the Temple Mount. There Abraham, Moses, and Jesus confirmed him as the "seal of a prophet."

In Muhammad's thoughts and emotions the Temple Mount was a special place of divine revelation and the gate to heaven. Islamic tradition considers it the arena of the last judgment and the place to which the Messiah (*Al Mahdi*) will return.

At the end of time, Muslims believe that the Kaaba will even be brought from Mecca to Jerusalem where, united with the rock of Moriah, it will form the foundation stone for the new world. It is no coincidence that Jerusalem is the only city which Islam calls "the holy one," *Al Kuds.*

The battle against the Jews

Muhammad sought new ways to anchor his message apart from Jews and Christians, in order to avoid their derision. He clearly feared he would lose his standing as prophet and his honor among the Arabs, which was based on the assumption of divine revelation.

Consequently Muhammad struggled against Jews with all his might. The tribes were subjugated, enslaved, banished, or exterminated. He thought his victory over the Jews proved that God had made him lord and judge over Jews and Christians. He viewed himself as the son and successor of Abraham, who long before the Jews and Christians was the most important prophet and the "first Muslim."

Abraham as key person

Abraham, the central figure for Jews and Christians, became Muhammad's proof and anchor for the primacy of Islam. In sura 3:60 and 62 we read, *"Abraham was not a Jew nor a Christian; but he was a god-fearing Hanif* [Muslim] *and no heathen. The persons closest to Abraham are those who follow him, and this prophet* [Muhammad], *and those who believe with him."*

Sura 2:134, *"Or will you say that Abraham, Ishmael, Isaac, Jacob and the tribes were Jews or Christians? Do you know better than Allah?"* Abraham becomes a Muslim because according to Islam he lived a godly life, namely "Islam."

Muhammad soon realized that he could not do without Mecca, the religious center, if Islam were to seize and control all the Arab tribes. Thus Mecca was not simply conquered; the religious cult of the Kaaba was given Islamic meaning and made the magnet of Islamic pilgrimage.

It was absolutely necessary for Muhammad to connect Abraham with the Kaaba as well. Sura 3:90 and 91: *"The first house of Allah, made for me, is the one in Mecca . . . for blessing and guidance to all people. In it are clear signs: it is the holy place of Abraham."*

In this way Muhammad attempted to distance himself from Jerusalem and the Jews. Sura 2:119–123, *"At that time, when we*

made the house of Kaaba for a place of asylum for men ... we
required of Abraham and Ishmael, 'cleanse my house...' At that
time, when Abraham and Ishmael laid the foundations of the Kaaba,
they said, 'O our Lord, receive it from us and make us Muslims and a
people submitted to Allah ... and let an Apostle arise from among
their midst ... to instruct them in scripture and wisdom...' "

This attempt was unsuccessful and never convinced even
Muhammad himself. Although the Koran proclaimed that Allah
supported Muhammad and approved the change of prayer
direction from Jerusalem to Mecca in a special revelation,
Muhammad knew that Jerusalem would remain connected
with Abraham's name. This was so even if Abraham was
declared the founder of the Kaaba in Mecca.

In addition, Jerusalem was not then within his scope.
Therefore the Kaaba, which allegedly had been built by
Abraham and Ishmael as a house of prayer, was turned into
the first house of Allah, which was built for mankind itself.
In the same way Islam identified itself as the original, natural
religion for all of mankind.

According to this doctrine, Allah used Abraham to teach
Islam to mankind. Simultaneously, Abraham became the first
to prophesy Muhammad's coming. He predicted the formation of the true (that is, the Islamic) congregation under
Muhammad's leadership.

However, it was not only Abraham whom Muhammad
enlisted in Islam's service, but all of Israel's patriarchs.

Sura 2:134: *"Or will you say that Abraham, Ishmael, Jacob ...*
were Jews or Christians? Say, Do you know better than Allah? And
they said No! For us there is none of them who added other gods to
the one Allah. We believe in Allah and the revelation sent down to us
and to Abraham and Ishmael ... we make no difference between
one and another of them; truly we are Muslims."

How could Muhammad claim that Abraham and the
patriarchs were all Muslims? According to the Koran (sura

30:30) every person is a Muslim. In addition, according to Muhammad, Judaism began at Sinai and Christianity with Christ.

Following this logic, Abraham and the patriarchs were neither Jews nor Christians, but Muslims. Moses, David, Solomon, and Jesus are also made into Islamic prophets. Muhammad thus "returned" all religious history to Islam.

Judaism and Christianity as "falsified messages"

This means that according to the Koran, Judaism and Christianity are nothing but falsified, disconnected, perverted Islamic messages.

Allah sent the Islamic prophet Moses to the Jews to proclaim that they were chosen to walk in the footsteps of the Islamic patriarch and prophet Abraham; they were to take the godly patriarchs as examples. They should have been an exemplary people by obeying Allah's commands. But they rejected, persecuted, and killed the prophets who were sent to them, thus demonstrating their evil, wicked nature.

As disobedient unbelievers, then, the Jews are assumed to have forfeited their election. They were damned by Allah (sura 4:46) and turned over to Islamic society, primarily Muhammad as Allah's prophet and representative, for judgment and discipline.

Jesus "prophesied the coming of Muhammad"

According to Muslim theology, Jesus also, the second-most important Islamic prophet, taught nothing but pure Islam and even prophesied Muhammad's coming. But the Christians distorted and perverted his message, suppressing much of it. Therefore the Christian fellowship ended up with a blasphemous, religiously perverted and limited confession.

"Allah has no son and Jesus was not crucified," is Islam's message to the Christian Church. Sura 4:157–158: *"But in reality they neither killed him nor crucified him, but they exchanged him for another – no he was not killed, but Allah raised him up to himself in heaven."*

Sura 5:72: *"They are not believers who say that Allah is Christ the son of Mary."*

According to Islam, Christ's followers also failed, so Allah chose a new fellowship for himself, one according to his heart. He found it in the Arab people, in Muhammad and his followers. Sura 3:110: *"Ye [Muslims] are the best of peoples, evolved for mankind, enjoining what is right, forbidding what is wrong, and believing in Allah. If only the People of the Book had faith, it were best for them."*

Islam's territorial thinking

Allah turned everything over to this new Muslim fellowship: the election, the holy land, the calling. He chose them to be the exemplary people who are closest to him. If then the majority of the biblical prophets are declared Muslims (even David and Solomon), the land where these prophets lived and worked is naturally Islamic land.

For example, to Muslims Bethlehem is an Islamic town because Jesus, the second-most important Islamic prophet, was born there; Nazareth is Islamic because he spent his childhood there; Hebron is Islamic because the Islamic patriarchs Abraham, Isaac, and Jacob are buried there; Jerusalem is Islamic because it was the city of the Islamic prophets David and Solomon and because Muhammad himself went to heaven from the Temple Mount.

Islam thinks in terms of territory. The world must be conquered and brought under the rule of divine law because wherever Islam rules the world is as Allah desires. To bring peoples under Islam's reign is to bring them into the natural condition which Allah intended from the beginning. Since Islam is the natural religion of mankind, a non-Muslim lives in an unnatural condition, unacceptable to Allah. Nothing better can happen to a person than to be brought under Islam's reign.

In spite of all the assertions that Islam is a "religion of peace" whose nature includes possibilities for reconciliation, we must perceive Islam as it perceives itself. It does not see itself as a religion on a level with other religions. It seeks neither co-existence nor parity with other religions. It co-exists with others only when it lacks the power to reign, according to the motto, "The hand you cannot cut off you must shake."

Islam claims a leading position as the natural, original religion, after the wretched failure of other religions, especially Judaism and Christianity. Allah confirmed it through his prophet Muhammad as the sole religion which is untainted, healthy, and pleasing to him (sura 7:158 and 3:110).

Because Allah confirmed that Islam is the only right religion (sura 9:33: *"It is he who sent his apostle with the true religion in order to make it victorious over everything ... "*) he also appointed it to rule. He gave the Islamic fellowship the task of subjecting the whole world to Islam's reign. Therefore Islam divides the world into two territories: the house of Islam (i.e. "peace") and the house of war.

Dar al-islam, house of peace

The "house of peace" is the area where Islam physically reigns.

Muslims and non-Muslims are not given the same rights. If Jews and Christians do not convert to Islam they are allowed to live, but as second-class persons, so-called "protected ones." The Islamic ruler should protect them from the justified wrath of Allah and Islamic society. But they are differentiated from

Muslims by special taxes, by lack of rights in court, by exclusion from public office, and by humiliating positions in society. Their beliefs are a tolerated blemish on Allah and Islamic society.

Of course, at some times and under some Islamic rulers, the Jews and Christians were treated more humanely, e.g. in Spain under the Moors. But the Koran itself and the traditions make it perfectly clear how Jews and Christians are to be treated. For the heathen there was the choice only of conversion to Islam or death (sura 9:5: *"slay them . . . "*).

Dar al-harb, house of war

The second territory is called the "house of war," i.e. all those nations and peoples which are not yet under Islam's reign. Islam's attitude toward this territory was and is very simple. It must be fought until it is subjected to Islam. Every area on earth which is not under Allah's (Islam's) reign, offends him and must sooner or later be punished.

Muslims' call to battle is not, as it is often harmlessly presented, a spiritual matter but a very concrete order to fight for Islam with the sword. Muhammad himself is called to take up the sword to fight and kill. Sura 8:65: *"Prophet, lead the believers to the fight. If there are 20 among you who persevere they will overcome 200 . . . "*

Further texts on this subject are Sura 8:67: *"No prophet may have prisoners of war and set them free for money as long as the opponents in the land are not completely subdued"*; Sura 9:14: *"When you fight them . . . "*; Sura 9:123: *"Fight those who are near you . . . so that they see you can be firm . . . "*; Sura 47:4, 48:29, 2:216ff.: *"You must fight against the unbelievers . . . "*

An additional reason for fighting the unbelievers is their opposition to Muhammad. Sura 8:12–13: *"I will instill terror into the unbelievers, smite them with the sword . . . that will be their punishment ... that they have opposed Allah and his apostle – see how strict Allah punishes."*

In order to motivate Muslims to battle, not only are the unwilling threatened with punishment, but those who participate are enticed materially with part of the enemies' plunder. (Of course Muhammad had precedence and received the lions' share.)

Sura 8:41: *"And know that when you take any booty, a fifth share is assigned to Allah and to the apostle, and to relatives, orphans, the needy the wayfarer, and to him who has become needy because he followed Allah."*

Sura 4:94: *"Allah gives you enough ways to make plunder... ";* 95: *"Allah granted great reward to those who fight in war";* 8:1: *"They ask concerning the plunder of war. They are for Allah and the apostle."*

Islam and Western thought

According to the Koran, the Islamic community claims the possessions of unbelievers and heathen who do not convert to Islam and who are therefore killed or treated as second-class persons. This concept that possessions, including land, wives, and children (whom Islam considers the man's possessions) are transferred to the hand of the victor may sound archaic to Western ears. But it is Islamic thinking through and through.

Islam considers everything its possession wherever an Islamic ruler sets his foot, dwells, or buries his dead, because this establishes Allah's claim to the land.

It is extremely difficult for Jews and Christians, in fact for all non-Muslims, to understand such a different way of thinking. This is not simply a matter of diverse morals, ethics, or perception of right and wrong. These are more fundamental differences, a wholly different starting point, a different foundation of logic, perception, and reality.

This has nothing to do with intelligence, education, or cultural background. This totally different understanding of God and of man not only results in a very different understanding of truth, but also a different relationship to reality.

We have a personal God who seeks relationships

Jews and Christians believe in a God who not only created the world, but has a continuing relationship to it and actively participates in man's history. He reveals himself in a concrete way in time and space, and in man's history. He intervenes visibly and tangibly in man's daily life.

God reveals himself in history as a Father who disciplines and corrects his sons because he is interested in truth in the innermost parts and in a personal heart relationship. We see this in his encounters with Abraham, Jacob, and Moses; in Israel's exodus from Egypt to the Promised Land; in God's instruction, encouragement, admonishment, warning, healing, judging; in the renewed forgiveness through the words of his prophets; in scattering and banishment; in the gathering and restoration of Israel.

In the new covenant, in the incarnation of his Son the Messiah Jesus, God's truth (he is love) and his grace (his love is for me) are revealed. God descends into time and space and becomes a part of man's history.

In the Bible, both the old and the new covenant speak of God's salvation history, which has a beginning and an end. God reveals himself in both individual and collective history. He himself challenges human beings not to forget his redemptive interventions in history.

> "... when your son asks you ... tell him: 'We were slaves of Pharaoh in Egypt, but the LORD brought us out of Egypt with a mighty hand.'"   (Deuteronomy 6:20–21)

Allah is outside history

Historical thinking is indispensable for Jews and Christians. Our relationship to reality orients itself by what happens in time and space.

This is not the case with Islam, where a personal, intimate relationship between Allah and humanity, as between father and child, is unseemly and inconceivable because Allah cannot be thought of as contiguous with weak and sinful men. The honor and majesty of the endlessly exalted Allah would be profaned and stained by inappropriate proximity to a man, even the prophet.

Therefore, according to Islam, Allah cannot participate in human history. That Allah could humble himself and take on the form of a servant, as Philippians 2 says of God, submitting like a man to the law of time and space, of transience, pain, and death is absolutely blasphemous to Islamic thought. The god of Islam confronts man with his law, not with himself. We can speak of Islam as a religion with an "absent god."

The starting point for all Muslim thought and logic is the word revealed through Muhammad in the Koran and in the traditions regarding Muhammad's life. Because Allah is outside history his word has no relationship to man's history. A Muslim cannot question revealed law, the word of Allah in the Koran, because it is absolutely binding truth. Every message which does not conform to it is branded a lie, falsification, and godlessness.

Therefore the former Saudi King Feisal said of the Jewish claim to the Temple Mount, "Archeology has not yet convincingly proven that the Jewish temple ever stood there." (This accords with Islam's teaching that the Bible has been tampered with; in addition, non-Muslim historians and archaeologists can provide only "falsifications.") Feisal continued, "But from divine revelation we know that the prophet Muhammad rode to Jerusalem on his winged horse in order to ascend to heaven from that place."

Islamic logic

Some time ago Sheikh Salah Ra'ad, former mayor of Um-Al-Fahm in Israel and recognized Islam authority among Israeli Arabs, was asked what he thought about the Jewish claim to the Temple Mount and the Western Wall.

He replied, "The Jews' claim to the Temple Mount and the Western Wall is incorrect and misleading thinking. The Jews have absolutely no right to the Temple Mount area or to even a single stone of the Al Aksa Mosque. Archaeologists have clearly proven that the Alburak Wall [Islamic name for the Western Wall] has nothing to do with a Jewish temple. Unfortunately, Jewish extremists stir up Jewish emotions with lies and false information regarding the Temple Mount."

When asked about the historical reports of the temple in the Bible he replied, "We believe the Bible is falsified, not only regarding the history of the Temple. The Koran clearly teaches this."

Sheikh Salah Ra'ad was also asked, "Do you believe that seventy virgins are waiting in paradise as a reward for a martyr for Islam [suicide terrorist]?" The answer was, "We have clear proofs for this, as written in the Koran and in the *Sunna* [tradition of Muhammad's life]. The matter is clear: A martyr will receive six special rewards from Allah, including seventy virgins, he will not be tormented in the grave, and seventy of his relatives will enter paradise without passing judgment."

These examples of Islam's logic from an educated, moderate Muslim reveal its understanding of reality and truth. Terms such as truth, justice, even mercy and grace have a different content than in Judeo–Christian thought and faith.

We may use some of the same religious terms and even

claim common examples of faith (Abraham, Moses, Jesus), but the Bible's understanding of God and man has nothing in common with Islam's. All talk of the so-called common core and the similarity of monotheism is in the end misrepresentation, whether ignorance or intentional deception.

The Islamic world needs the Gospel

It is painful, demanding, and challenging to study Islam and find a clear biblical position. And yet Christians would be unloving and shirking their responsibility if we were to fail to bring Muslims the good news that God is not only their Creator, but also their Father and Savior.

For this reason we are challenged to look the differences in the eye. When we do so, we must testify that Islam as a religion is ultimately a strategic system which distorts God's true face and hinders access to personal fellowship with him as Father.

In closing I wish to stress once again that Muslims are not our enemies. According to Ephesians 6, our struggle is not against flesh and blood. As decidedly as we oppose Islam, we also decidedly respect and honor the people who live under its reign because the God of the Bible loves them and offers them salvation in Jesus as he does to us.

Chapter 3

Israel Today: the Near East Conflict from a Contemporary, Historical and Spiritual Standpoint

When considering the present conflict in and around Israel, it is important to understand the background and context and to be aware of God's purposes and plans for his people and for the nations. In view of the extremely one-sided media reports and the growth of worldwide anti-Semitism, it is urgent that the Church study this topic.

The world's eyes are on Israel

The whole world's eyes are on Israel. The leaders of important countries and the United Nations are dropping everything to urgently seek a solution to the so-called Israel–Palestinian conflict, using pressure, threats and money. It seems as if the leaders of this world consider it a personal challenge to solve this problem; they deal with it as though they were defusing a bomb which would cause worldwide destruction if it exploded.

There is no question that Israel, especially Jerusalem, has pivotal significance in the world. Even Shimon Peres, an Israeli politician, suggests making Jerusalem the world capital which would be ruled directly from the UNO by the General Secretary himself. Whatever happens in Israel and Jerusalem obviously stirs everyone, not only Jews and Muslims.

In the midst of this bloody and insolvable conflict, one could be grateful for the world community's attention, instead of living in isolation. However, this attention often proves counter-productive, causing Israel disappointment and even pain.

The UNO general assembly's resolutions which unreservedly condemn Israel as the aggressor and guilty party have confirmed the simple black and white picture propagated by the mass media in the whole world, especially Europe.

Israel and the Jews are portrayed as the occupier who suppresses, mistreats and kills the Arabs in the autonomous areas, refusing them the legitimate right to their land and their capital Jerusalem. The media show tanks against stone-throwing children, youths and women, with many more dead and wounded on the Arab side compared with the Israelis. Moving pictures of young people dying in their fathers' arms are sent around the world.

The angry and hate-filled cry of the crowds in all the Arab countries is for revenge, retaliation and a holy war to liberate Islamic land, which means all of Israel. The West and many other nations add their voices to this enraged cry for justice. In the opinion of the world community, especially Europe, Israel is hindering and refusing the Palestinian Arabs their legitimate right to their own country.

Palestinians under Jordanian and Egyptian rule

It is very quickly forgotten that between 1948 and 1967, a period of almost twenty years, the West Bank and East Jerusalem were ruled by Jordan, and Gaza was ruled by Egypt. Neither of these nations granted their Palestinian brothers the right even to autonomous administration, let alone their own state. On the contrary, in the early 1970s a Palestinian uprising in Jordan, known as Black September, was quelled with tanks. It left thousands dead; Arafat and his followers had to flee the country.

In several Arab countries the Palestinians have been mistreated and considered second-class persons. Was there ever a voice raised in the West about this? This is not a matter of pushing responsibility for the current Palestinian problem on the Arab nations, but it is important to correctly understand the roots of this conflict. We Christians especially should look for truth and not let ourselves be influenced by emotional, dishonest reporting in the media.

Israel and the Jewish people are often portrayed by the UNO as the source of evil and the reason for Palestinian Arabs' distress. Only a few countries oppose this; apart from the United States, most of them are small nations such as Micronesia. Others either concur in the condemnation of Israel or belong to the silent crowd. This is nothing new in Jewish history.

Jews – perpetrators or victims?

One cannot help but think that it is not entirely unwelcome for many to see Israel branded in this way because it eases their consciences; it provides a way to escape responsibility for their own miserable history as perpetrators of offences against the Jewish people. Justice is indignantly demanded for the victims who for once are not Jews. The West's desire to leave behind its own gruesome and dark history with the Jewish people may be so great that its perception of today's situation is massively clouded.

Children misused

Let's take a closer look at the reality of the situation as it is experienced here, e.g. children and youths throwing stones at tanks and rubber bullets. According to CNN, which represents the Western media, this is a battle between a heavily armed army and unarmed, defenseless women and children who take to the streets to struggle with their bare hands for survival and freedom. Apart from the Queen of Sweden, no one seems to have noticed that children and youths are strategically misused and sacrificed.

We have first-hand knowledge of children from Arab–Christian backgrounds who have been forced to participate in the uprising by throwing stones, under threat of being branded as traitors if they refuse. Other children or youths, who themselves have been incited by their religious or national leaders, teachers, or even their own parents, goad them to participate.

Thus, driven by a mixture of fear of their own people, a sense of nationalistic honor or the prospect of reward in paradise, as taught by Islam, these youngsters are willing to risk their lives. As further inducement, the PLO pays every family $2,000 for each person killed in the uprising and $300 for every wounded person.

Almost every Friday the call goes out from the mosques to sacrifice one's life in order to destroy the Jews and liberate all of Palestine, which is considered holy Islamic ground. "All Palestine" refers to the whole of present-day Israel, from Galilee in the north to the Negev in the south. It is no coincidence that Israel is nowhere to be found in the school-books issued this year by the Palestinian Authority.

Call to holy war

The following quote from a sermon given in the Zayed bin Sultan Al Nahyan Mosque in Gaza on October 13, 2000, shows clearly how the emotions and thoughts of Palestinian Arabs, especially youths and children, are influenced daily.

"The Jews are Jews, whether Labor or Likud ... They have no moderates and no peace mediators. They are all liars...

O brothers in faith, the criminals, the terrorists are the Jews who mow down our children or make them orphans and our women widows, as well as defiling our holy places. They are the terrorists. They are the ones who must be mown down and killed, as Allah the almighty said, 'Fight them. Allah will let them be tortured by your hands, will humiliate them, will help you overcome them and will rejuvenate the believers' senses...'

We are fighting, killing and being killed on the path of Allah; such are the costs and the dowry of the bride, the dowry from paradise. Allah bought the persons and possessions of the believers, giving them in return his promise that they will possess paradise, for they fight for Allah, they slaughter the enemy and are slaughtered. That is a promise from him [Allah], as described in the Old Testament, the Gospel and the Koran...

The Jews are allied with the Christians, and the Christians with the Jews, in spite of the enmity between them. The enmity between the Jews and Christians is deep but they are united against the monotheists who say, 'There is no God but Allah and Muhammad is his prophet.' In other words, they are opposed to you, O Muslims...

Although a treaty was signed for Gaza, we will not forget Haifa and Acco, Galilee and Jaffa and the triangle and the Negev and the rest of our cities and villages. It is only a matter of time ... Have no mercy on the Jews, wherever they are, in whatever countries. Fight them wherever you are. Wherever you encounter them, kill them. Wherever you are, kill these Jews and these Americans who are like them."

(Translated from Arabic by the Middle East Media Research Institute)

During the weekend beginning October 13, this sermon was broadcast several times on Palestinian TV. Every Friday sermons like this can be heard in many mosques, including the El Aksa Mosque on the Temple Mount. As far as we know, the Western media have not discussed this hate-filled call to murder and destruction, nor have the UNO or representatives of Western governments taken a stand against it.

Yasser Arafat can get by with saying in a public interview regarding the Israeli Prime Minister, "Go to hell", without upsetting people or being interpreted as lacking the will for peace.

The Egyptian Secretary of State publicly identified himself with the goals of Hamas and Jihad, calling them the common goal of all Arabs, without an international outcry or even questions asked. And Hamas' goals are generally known, i.e. destroying the Jewish state and driving the Jews out of Islamic territory.

Not an ethnic conflict

One can speak here of a distorted perception of the conflict. It is not up to our Community of Reconciliation to take sides, but to stand for the truth. We are friends of both the Jewish and the Arab peoples. We identify with God's promises to the Jewish people now and to his history with them, as his Word testifies. But we are just as concerned for the Arabs' well-being, salvation and peace.

Just because of that, it important for us to point out that this is not simply an ethnic conflict or even a battle between two peoples for the same land, which is only the smallest part of the truth. Had this been the case, the Arab Palestinians could already have had their own homeland and state more than fifty years ago, when both the UN and the Jews offered it to them. However, their own Arab brothers prevented them from taking it.

Jordan and Egypt divided the land at that time but had no interest in giving the Palestinian Arabs any degree of autonomy. On the contrary, in 1964 when East Jerusalem, the West Bank and Gaza were in Jordanian and Egyptian hands, the PLO came into being under the patronage of King Hussein and President Nasser. Yasser Arafat did not arrive on the scene until four years later.

The PLO's goal, according to the battle cry at that time, was to drive the Jews into the sea and liberate all of Palestine, i.e. to eradicate Israel. This goal is still recorded in the PLO charter, in spite of the Oslo Accords.

Islam's claims to Israel and Jerusalem

What am I trying to say here? The point is that it is not ultimately a matter of the fate and desire of the Palestinian Arabs. Islam claims the whole of Israel, which is considered to be holy Islamic land, especially Jerusalem and the Temple Mount. For Islam it is unbearable that the Jews rule over Islamic land and have sovereignty over the Temple Mount.

According to the Koran, the Jewish people are rejected by God and given over to the Muslims for judgment and destruction. The history of the Jews during the last two thousand years confirms the Muslim view that Jews are the scum of the world, persecuted by all the nations, destroyed and eventually vomited onto Islamic soil. To be sure, the Muslims will never forgive the West for this last point.

Islam versus the biblical, Judeo–Christian revelation of God

The existence of the nation of Israel and the presence of the Jewish people in the land are a threat to Islam and to Muslims. This questions Islam's understanding of itself as the ruling religion which possesses the ultimate truth.

We must not forget that for almost 1,400 years Jerusalem and the so-called Holy Land were almost uninterruptedly under Islamic rule. But when the Jews returned, they demanded this sovereignty and reiterated their claim to Jerusalem.

This is the age-old battle of election. Has the Islamic community replaced the Jews as God's chosen people, as his instrument for bringing his kingdom to the world, or has it not? Who has the truth, the authority and the rule – Islam or the biblical, Jewish–Christian revelation of God? According to Islam the authority belongs to him who rules over the Temple Mount.

We do not wish to distract attention from the distress of those caught up in this conflict, but to indicate its real source. We must not get stuck in the surface events and pass by the truth.

Chapter 4

God's View of the Whole Near East

The Near East – a center of blessing (Isaiah 19:24–25)

In chapter 19 of the prophet Isaiah, God promised to make the Near East a center of blessing. But what is his strategy for fulfilling his prophecies?

As a result of the Israeli–Palestinian conflict, the situation in the Near East and the relationship between Jews and Arabs have become the quintessence of irreconcilability, hatred and violence. In hundreds of conflicts and violent struggles all over the world, much more blood is often shed. But the Near East conflict is one which arouses emotions everywhere. Everyone, whether asked or not, feels obliged to offer his opinion.

This conflict has already brought many Israeli, Arab, and international peace movements, heads of state, politicians, and other mediators to the limits of their energy, gifts, and options. The only person who was able to achieve limited success, through an unbelievably courageous act, paid for it with his life. The former Egyptian President Sadat made a peace treaty with Israel in 1979 and was assassinated by his own people. Since then his success has been slowly eroded away.

According to a European survey in 2003 (before the Iraq war), Iraq is now considered the greatest threat to world peace and Israel the second-greatest. It is said that the Near East has the potential to detonate the entire world.

Treatment of the Near East conflict is unique, both on the personal emotional level and on the international political level. Western and Eastern Europeans, Americans, Asians and Africans dance around it on various political stages, attempting to trump each other with suggested solutions. But so far not one of these proposals has been implemented.

Jerusalem the stumbling stone

Every attempt at reconciliation and every peace initiative breaks down on the fact that both the Jewish people and Islam link their identity, their home, and their inheritance with Jerusalem, more precisely with the Temple Mount, where God revealed himself. Neither Jews nor Muslims can relinquish this place to the other without giving up themselves.

Many in the West think that Jerusalem is merely the Muslims' third-holiest city. But it means much more to Islam. I will give just a few of the reasons for this.

Approximately eighteen years after Islam was established in Medina, Jerusalem was taken by Caliph Omar, Muhammad's successor. The bishop of Jerusalem, Patriarch Sophoronius, gave Omar the Temple Mount in order to build an Islamic place of prayer (mosque) there. Christians had made the Temple Mount a garbage dump in order to verify – through a conscious desecration of the holy places – the widely held dogma of God's rejection of the Jewish people.

Omar cleaned the Temple Mount and built the Al Aksa Mosque there because sura 17 of the Koran says that Muhammad rode to the "distant prayer place" (*Al Aksa*) one night on his winged horse. It also says he was taken into heaven from there in order to be installed as head of all the prophets. That could not be done in Mecca or Medina because only Jerusalem was the city of the prophets.

That is why the first Muslims prayed toward Jerusalem, not Mecca. A special revelation was necessary to permit and justify their later turning toward Mecca. This was actually a political maneuver whose goal was to bring Mecca (in pre-Islamic times the seat of Arabian power) under Islamic reign.

The meaning of Jerusalem for Islam and for Judaism

But Jerusalem has a central role in Islamic theology of end-time events. For Islam it is the city of the prophets and of Allah's revelation. It is no coincidence that this is the only city which Islam names *Al Kuds*, the Holy One. Whoever possesses it belongs to the succession of prophets, to Allah's chosen, to the true believers, to the people whom Allah has given sovereignty over this world.

For Jews, Jerusalem is quite plainly the center, the origin, and the fulfillment of their identity and destiny as a people and a nation. That is why for 2,000 years all Jews have expressed their longing by concluding the Seder evening (the eve of the first day of Passover) with the wish and prayer, "Next year in Jerusalem."

By Jerusalem, I mean the Temple Mount, where Solomon's temple stood. At its dedication, the God of Israel descended in his holiness and sanctified the place for all time, declaring, *"My eyes and my heart will always be there"* (1 Kings 9:3; see also 8:10–13).

Israel is called to live in the presence of its God and to be a people of priests and a light to the nations. It cannot attain rest, peace, and the fulfillment of its destiny except by returning to God's presence, by *aliyah* ("go up," modern Hebrew for the immigration of Jews to Israel).

This means going up to the temple on the Temple Mount,

into the presence of God. God has bound Israel's calling and inheritance to this land, specifically to this place.

Israel's calling

It is Israel's calling to live according to God's revelation, in order to make him known to the world. From the presence of him who is the light of the world, Israel should bring light to the nations:

> *"Arise, shine, for your light has come,*
> *and the glory of the LORD rises upon you.*
> *See, darkness covers the earth*
> *and thick darkness is over the peoples,*
> *but the LORD rises upon you*
> *and his glory appears over you.*
> *Nations will come to your light,*
> *and kings to the brightness of your dawn."*
>
> (Isaiah 60:1–3)

The majority of the Jewish people – and the state of Israel itself – have not yet come into this light or the promised presence of God. But God is nevertheless at work restoring Israel as a people and a nation, in order to bring it into its inheritance. Then his glory will be revealed and his name made holy among the nations.

This is about Israel in regard to the honor of God and his salvation for the nations (Ezekiel 36:31–38). And yet Israel can enter its calling only in the place determined by God. According to his Word, the land and people belong together in such a way that the Diaspora, life outside the land of Israel, demonstrates God's judgment on Israel and his distance from them.

If the Jews do not want to lose or give up their identity and calling as a people – and they are a people only insofar as they are

God's people – they must return to Israel, to Zion, to Jerusalem. For only there will God come to his people as a people.

The roots of the Near East conflict

These are the hopelessly tangled roots of the Near East conflict. The nations – and often some Israeli leaders themselves – see this as a political, ethnic, human and cultural problem which could be solved with sensible suggestions and compromises. Although they themselves see the Sisyphean nature of their efforts, they don't realize that this is more than a struggle of two peoples for the same land or for historic rights and independence. It is a battle for identity and destiny, a battle for election and inheritance.

As central as Jerusalem is for the Jewish people and the fulfillment of the biblical promise, so it is for Islam as well. Islam clearly confesses and clings to the belief that Allah honored the Islamic community with the final revelation of truth, calling it to bring the world under Islam's rule. Jerusalem, the city of the prophets, is a symbol of Islamic rule which must not be forfeited.

Nothing threatens Islam's identity and supremacy more than seeing Jerusalem in the hands of Jews who, according to the Koran and Islamic tradition, are rejected and cursed by Allah. Ruling over the Temple Mount symbolizes and legitimizes Allah's election and the call to be his witness.

There is no doubt that the Koran teaches that this election through Abraham and Ishmael applies solely to Muslims, primarily the Arab people. There is no such thing as reconciliation with non-Muslims.

The biblical view

The biblical view is different. God promises the prophet Isaiah (19:24–25) that the day will come when he will cleanse Egypt,

Assyria (which then comprised what is now the Arab part of the Near East) and Israel through his judgment. He will break their pride, reconcile them to each other, and bind them together in order to make them a corporate blessing on earth.

God has given us a glimpse of a currently unimaginable future, namely that nations such as Syria, Iraq, Saudi Arabia and Egypt will one day make a covenant with Israel. This covenant will be a blessing not only for them, but for the whole world.

And God never speaks empty words! In Numbers 23:19 we read,

> *"God is not a man, that he should lie,*
> *nor a son of man, that he should change his mind.*
> *Does he speak and then not act?"*

God's promise to make the Near East a center of blessing has to do with his faithfulness toward Abraham. The Arab peoples – as descendants of Ishmael, Abraham's son "according to the flesh" – were promised a blessing for Abraham's sake (Genesis 21:13–20).

Blessing always means fullness of life and fruitfulness in all areas, peace, freedom, salvation. But the descendants of Ishmael are called not only to receive blessings, but to be a blessing together with Israel (Isaiah 19:24). I believe they have a meaningful calling both for the Church and for the nations.

We are not desperately seeking a special calling for the Arab people in order to reconcile them with the Jewish people. Any people can be reconciled with itself, with its own destiny, with its neighbor and with God only when it recognizes the God of Israel in the face of the crucified Jesus of Nazareth. He must be seen as the one who is love, who is absolutely good, true and just.

Every calling and every election which God pronounces can in the end – providing it is fulfilled through obedience – bring forth nothing but salvation, peace and joy, both for the one who is called and for all others and the whole creation. For in his will lies our salvation, our life, our joy.

Therefore in God's kingdom we can never weigh callings and elections against each other. Whoever does that does not really know God! We as the Church of Jesus want to sensitively listen to God's word in order to understand how he sees Ishmael's descendants. Then we will be able to encourage them in their calling.

Blessing for Ishmael

First of all we wish to make clear that Ishmael, even though born of Abraham's disobedience and lack of faith, was accepted and affirmed by God. Because he was circumcised by Abraham he participated in the covenant God made with Abraham, for even after the necessary banishment – or rather, his separation from Isaac – God personally cared for Ishmael.

This separation, as painful and traumatic as it must have been for both Abraham and Ishmael, was unavoidable. Isaac was the fulfillment of God's plans with Abraham, not Ishmael, who was born of Abraham's will. God's plans cannot be manipulated by men because only what is born of his will brings salvation to his creation.

And yet God's mercy by far exceeds all our comprehending and understanding! First, he can transform all our mistakes into blessings, providing they are laid in his hands. Second, we read in Psalm 37:4,

> "Delight yourself in the LORD
> and he will give you the desires of your heart."

Abraham, the friend of God, who made honoring God the highest priority in his life (Romans 4:20–21), had the desires of his heart fulfilled, even though he was not spared the pain of separation.

In Genesis 17:18 Abraham asked, *"If only Ishmael might live under your blessing!"* After God once again made clear that he had not changed his plans for Isaac (i.e. to establish the special covenant with him), nor would he change them, he promised Abraham,

> *"As for Ishmael, I have heard you: I will surely bless him; I will make him fruitful and will greatly increase his numbers ... I will make the son of the maidservant into a nation also, because he is your offspring."*
>
> (Genesis 17:20; 21:13)

God gave the reason for his promise, *"...because he is your offspring."*

In his goodness and his mercy, God not only heard the heart's desire of his friend, but also cared for the needs of the maidservant, Hagar. Her heart was a mixture of helplessness, wretchedness and pride, but she was without rights. She had done nothing to become a part of this story of disobedience. Even though pride caused part of her misery, she was still one of the wretched little ones whom God picks up out of the dust.

Thus the angel of the Lord visited her personally in order to bring the name of her son and convey the promise of blessing regarding him (Genesis 16:10–11). What unbelievable dignity this bestowed on the maidservant, Ishmael's mother! The name of her son would be Ishmael, *"God hears."*

Later when Ishmael and his mother were sent away from Abraham's house, leaving them homeless and fatherless, God took care of the boy and his mother, as we read in Genesis 21:17,

> *"God heard the boy crying, and the angel of God called to Hagar from heaven and said to her, 'What is the matter,*

Hagar? Do not be afraid; God has heard the boy crying as he lies there.'"

God did not want the boy to die. As he had promised with the boy's name, he listened to Ishmael's voice and intervened in order to save him in the desert. Again God spoke to Hagar, gave her water and confirmed that he wanted to give Ishmael a great future.

Ishmael's character

Ishmael's character was described even before his birth, in Genesis 16:12:

> *"He will be a wild donkey of a man;*
>   *his hand will be against everyone*
> *and everyone's hand against him,*
>   *and he will live in hostility*
>   *toward all his brothers."*

This already predicts some of the struggles and battles which now painfully characterize the relationship between the un-equal brothers. It often causes us to forget that just as God remained faithful to Isaac through all his disobedience, falling away and godlessness; just as he let nothing deter him from his promises and plans for Isaac – likewise he will allow nothing to keep him from fulfilling his promise to Ishmael, for he is one and the same God!

To be sure, Ishmael had to leave the father's house (every-thing which is born of man's will must be removed from the father's house), but he was not abandoned. For it is written, *"God was with the boy"* (Genesis 21:20).

God never turned away from Ishmael – on the contrary! But he had to lead him into the desert because that is where God judges and corrects all "flesh." That is where God reveals the character of man, the depths of the human heart. In all Ishmael's independence, pride, stubbornness and trust in his own strength (symbolized by the wild olive tree growing rampantly), he grows under the eyes of God.

And God is allowing Ishmael to pass through times of drought and hunger, times of need and darkness, so that when he is at the end of his own power and ability he will again send up his cry for help to the God of his father Abraham. And the God of his father Abraham will hear him!

God will lead Ishmael's descendants out of the prison and darkness of Islam and bring them to the sole place where they will again see his face: Golgotha! He will bring them to the crucified one, the Lamb of God who bears the guilt and darkness of the world.

Here all flesh dies. Here all pride, all strength, all stubbornness is broken. Only here will Ishmael receive new access to his father's house. Only here, at the cross, will he hear God's voice again, saying to him, "You are no stranger, you are no longer expelled or rejected; you are my son and part of my family."

Ishmael will return home and sit at the table with Abraham, Isaac and Jacob; he will never be sent away again. To Abraham's joy, God will also glorify himself in Ishmael as truly as he, the living One, will glorify himself in Jacob and in Israel!

I sense from God's Word that when Ishmael finds his way back home through the Messiah Jesus, his calling will begin to unfold.

Excursus: The prophetic picture of the olive tree

Before we further consider Ishmael's calling, I want to present an interpretation of the olive tree. I interpret the picture of the olive tree as follows:

From the fruit of the olive tree, oil is pressed. In the Bible oil is a symbol of the Holy Spirit. Therefore kings, prophets and priests were always anointed with oil. This made it clear that they were dedicated to God and did not receive office, honor and power in their own name, nor by the hand of the people, but solely by the hand of God and for his sake.

God is the source of power, he is the center and the goal of all human deeds, as we read in Colossians 1:16–17 regarding the Messiah, the Son of God,

> *"For by him all things were created: things in heaven and on earth, visible and invisible, whether thrones or powers or rulers or authorities; all things were created by him and for him. He is before all things, and in him all things hold together."*

Conversely, the anointing means that without the Holy Spirit, the person can do nothing which glorifies God's name. Only the Holy Spirit can cause the kind of fruit in us which reveals God's character.

Galatians 5:22–23 tells us,

> *"But the fruit of the Spirit is love, joy, peace, patience, kindness, goodness, faithfulness, gentleness and self-control."*

God is seeking this fruit of his Spirit in his people and in the nations because the essence of the calling and election of man is to reflect his glory!

The picture of the olive tree indicates that our history, our cultures, our traditions, our life and even our death have only the one goal. That is to bring forth the good oil through which God's holiness, his revelation, his love, truth and grace become visible.

The fall into sin poisoned the olive tree, which God had planted in Adam. The poison is arrogance, pride and disobedience. It made the tree grow rampantly and brought inedible, destructive, even deadly fruit.

We can see this destructive result in the story in Genesis. The flood washed away the evil poison but the Tower of Babel shows that the poisoned tree put out new shoots which again led human society to fall apart. The tree is incurably ill. The first olive tree was doomed to be a wild tree with a mortal illness (sin). It is written, *"The wages of sin is death"* (Romans 6:23).

The wild olive tree lives from the strength and the pride of man and is therefore under God's curse and judgment. In Jeremiah 17:5–6 we read,

"Cursed is the one who trusts in man,
  who depends on flesh for his strength
  and whose heart turns away from the LORD.
He will be like a bush in the wastelands;
  he will not see prosperity when it comes.
He will dwell in the parched places of the desert,
  in a salt land where no one lives."

But in human eyes this wild olive tree is not a bare bush in the wastelands, without fruit, but a tall, proud cedar. In Ezekiel 17:22–23 God refers to this cedar, promising that out of it a new, healthy and fruitful tree will be planted:

"This is what the Sovereign LORD says: I myself will take a shoot from the very top of a cedar and plant it; I will break off a tender sprig from its topmost shoots and plant it on a high and lofty mountain. On the mountain heights of Israel I will plant it; it will produce branches and bear fruit and become a splendid cedar."

With the calling of Abraham, a new tree was planted. The high and lofty mountain is Mount Moriah, or Mount Zion, where Abraham demonstrated his unconditional faith and obedience. God answered him – *"when the time had fully come"* – by sacrificing his own Son both for the salvation of the wild tree and for the fulfillment of all the promises to Abraham.

The new tree was planted in the ground of obedience and submission to the authority of the Messiah, who had already appeared to Abraham in the figure of Melchizedek. By giving a tithe of everything he had to Melchizedek, the king of Salem and high priest of the highest God, Abraham acknowledged Melchizedek's authority over himself and over all his descendants. Then he received the signs of the new covenant – bread and wine – from the hand of Melchizedek.

The fulfillment of the promises to Abraham (*"I will bless you and you will be a blessing"*) and the development of the new olive tree to full fruitfulness were from the beginning linked to the coming reign of the Messiah. They were anchored in the saving reality of the new covenant which Abraham, through his faith and obedience, already tasted prophetically!

This covenant was no longer made with the blood of animals, nor limited by the imperfect Aaronic priesthood, but – based on the holy blood of the Messiah himself – it opens unlimited access to the throne of God.

This is the new covenant which the prophet Jeremiah said would be written in our hearts (Jeremiah 31:31–34). This covenant is the inheritance of Jacob's descendants, the cultivated olive tree. It is also the inheritance of those who participate in Israel's history through the Messiah.

Abraham and the prophets – and with them all the God-fearing people in Israel – longed for this new covenant in the Messiah, the servant of God, Immanuel ("God with us"). They knew that only in him would the glory and the face of God be revealed in his people.

Without Yeshua ("God saves"), Israel can find neither its identity as a people nor its calling as the first-born. *He* is the key, *He* is the way, *He* is the door to the heart of Israel's God!

From the beginning God has worked on the olive tree Israel through his Word and his prophets. He pruned and disciplined it so that it would produce good fruit and good oil. But it was always just a remnant, a minority of the people, which brought forth the good oil of the revelation of God.

The Messiah and the olive tree

It was this holy remnant in the cultivated olive tree which ensured the presence of God and the flow of promises. It was also this remnant which *"when the time had fully come"* expected the Messiah and through faith perhaps even made his coming possible. (We think of Mary and Joseph, Zechariah and Elizabeth, Simeon and Anna, and many others in whom the presence of God was living.)

Through the Messiah, everything that precedes, that is, the history of both Israel and the nations is broken and pruned. Hearts are circumcised, not just the foreskin. He is the Cornerstone, the foundation on which Israel can build its house, according to the promise. He is the root and the offspring of David (Revelation 22:16) who anchors the cultivated olive tree Israel in God's heart and gives it eternal access to the springs of living water.

He will purify Israel, as written in Malachi 3:2–3,

> "... he will be like a refiner's fire or a launderer's soap. He will sit as a refiner and purifier of silver; he will purify the Levites and refine them like gold and silver. Then the LORD will have men who will bring offerings in righteousness."

He is the founder of a new human race. Only in him can Israel receive access to its own history and calling; only through him can Ishmael and the nations participate in Israel's history and calling to be a holy, fruitful *"kingdom of priests"* (the good oil) for their God (Exodus 19:6).

The olive tree symbolizes God's history with human beings, whose meaning and goal is to express his revelation, his presence and his being. The olive tree Israel cannot itself carry Ishmael and the nations. Only the Messiah carries Israel and through the purified and circumcised Israel, the nations as well.

The branches of Ishmael must be broken out of their history, culture and tradition, out of their ethnic and national circumstances. Like the rest of humanity they must be broken at the cross in order to be led back to the father's house through the Messiah Jesus and be grafted into God's history with Abraham.

Ishmael's calling

Isaiah is the prophet to whom God revealed the greatest portion of his salvation plans for the nations. He makes three important remarks about Ishmael's descendants, which I interpret as indications of Ishmael's calling. We find them in Isaiah 19:24–25, 42:10–12 and 60:6–7.

1. The praise and glorification of God in the whole world
Let us begin with Isaiah 42.

First the prophet describes the coming of the Messiah. He comes to proclaim the truth to the nations, to restore justice, to re-establish God's covenant with his people Israel and to be the light for the heathen. The blind receive their sight, prisoners are set free and the bound are led out of darkness. God creates new things: he restores Israel and leads nations out of darkness!

The whole creation is called to sing a new song to God, and the descendants of Ishmael are the first to be challenged by name.

> *"Sing to the L*ORD* a new song,*
>   *his praise from the ends of the earth,*
> *you who go down to the sea, and all that is in it,*
>   *you islands, and all who live in them.*
> *Let the desert and its towns raise their voices;*
>   *let the settlements where Kedar lives rejoice.*
> *Let the people of Sela sing for joy;*
>   *let them shout from the mountaintops.*
> *Let them give glory to the L*ORD
>   *and proclaim his praise in the islands."*
>
> (Isaiah 42:10–12)

Kedar, according to Genesis 25:13 and 1 Chronicles 1:29 was the second son of Ishmael, who like his father lived in the wilderness. In this way Ishmael is commanded to shout praises to God, to honor him and to proclaim his praise and glory on the islands (that is, among the nations).

When Ishmael recognizes the new thing God has created, he will break out in rejoicing because his homeless wandering in the desert has come to an end.

This rejoicing was already prophetically anticipated by an Arab, namely Jethro, Moses' Midianite father-in-law. After he saw the miracles God had done among the people of Israel, he broke out in rejoicing over this God of Israel. Then he placed his riches (i.e. his wisdom) at the disposal of Moses and the elders in a way which was revolutionary for Israel's leadership (Exodus 18).

2. Placing all riches at God's disposal

In chapter 60 Isaiah describes the glory of the Messiah who is enthroned in Jerusalem as king over his people Israel.

The peoples bring him their riches in order to pay homage to him.

Again Ishmael's descendants are named first.

> "Herds of camels will cover your land,
>   young camels of Midian and Ephah.
> And all from Sheba will come,
>   bearing gold and incense
>   and proclaiming the praise of the LORD.
> All Kedar's flocks will be gathered to you,
>   the rams of Nebaioth will serve you . . .
> The glory of Lebanon will come to you . . .
> to adorn the place of my sanctuary.

(Isaiah 60:6–7, 13)

The tribes mentioned here are all Arabian. It is as if Ishmael's descendants will lead the train of peoples to Jerusalem, to the Messiah and into the house of David!

3. A blessing of unity and reconciliation for the whole world

Therefore we cannot be surprised that in Isaiah 19:24–25, Isaiah proclaims the release of blessing for the whole world when the sons of Abraham are reconciled to each other:

> "In that day there will be a highway from Egypt to Assyria. The Assyrians will go to Egypt and the Egyptians to Assyria. The Egyptians and the Assyrians will worship together. In that day Israel will be the third, along with Egypt and Assyria, a blessing on the earth. The LORD Almighty will bless them, saying, 'Blessed be Egypt my people, Assyria my handiwork, and Israel my inheritance.'"

After the reconciliation of Isaac, the son of the promise, with Ishmael, the "son of the flesh," even Egypt, which was related to Abraham through the Egyptian woman Hagar, is included in the promise to be a blessing for the whole world.

The blessing which Abraham received from God, *"all peoples on earth will be blessed through you"* (Genesis 12:3), is fulfilled in the coming of Jesus, the Messiah, the Son and Lord of Abraham. In Isaiah 19:24–25, the prophet foresees that this blessing will flow out into the world through Abraham's united and reconciled family.

It is exactly because of this common, blessed future of Jews and Arabs that the adversary of God and hater of man comes into the picture. He attempts – thus far with some success – in all ways possible to hinder this reconciliation and uniting of Jews and Arabs.

Various walls of partition

One of the most powerful weapons of darkness is Islam. This is not only because Islamic lies shut Arabs' ears, eyes and hearts to the good news about Jesus, but also because they deny Israel's election.

Islam knows only one kind of relationship between Jews and Arabs – a relationship in which the Jews are so-called "protected ones" under Muslim rule and authority. The Jews are a people of Scriptures which in Islam's eyes have been tampered with. Although they are tolerated as subjects and second-class persons under Islamic rule, it would be absolutely unthinkable for them to live on a par with Muslims because from an Islamic standpoint the Jews are a people rejected and cursed by God.

Unfortunately, not only Arab Muslims think this way, but also a large part of Arab Christians. Although raised on Christian teaching, regarding the Jewish people's election they learn the same things as Muslims. They are also taught that Jews murdered the Messiah. In this way the enemy of God and man has built up a humanly invincible wall of division all around Jews and Arabs in order to prevent the release of God's blessing which would flow from unity.

The security wall which Israel is now building seems a visible manifestation of the spiritual wall of partition through the midst of Abraham's family! Israel's fear of Arabs is understandable. And yet it does not justify repeated demonstrations of scorn and discrimination toward the Arab people.

If the Messiah does not set Israel free from this attitude (and only he can do it), there will be adverse consequences. If the Arabs are not before all others welcomed in the house of Abraham, I fear that Israel's election and authority (both in the body of Christ and in the world) will not be developed to the full.

On the other hand, the Arab people will never attain rest, peace and identity as Abraham's children while they fail to turn away from hatred, enmity and violence. Their sometimes unbelievably arrogant attitude toward the Jewish people must come to an end. The Arab people must renounce the nationalism which destroys primarily itself, the nationalism born of Islam which poisons even Christian Arabs.

The Arab nationalism which wants to transform the land of Israel into an Islamic Palestine is destructive because it denies God's land promise to his people Israel. One can fight men, but not the plans and the will of God! In the long run, battling God destroys human existence.

God glorifies himself through broken vessels

God must humble, break and circumcise both Jews and Arabs in their inmost being, so that they can grow into the fullness of their calling in the house of their father Abraham.

Just as God has begun restoring the country of Israel, so must the reality of the Messiah, which is reconciliation through the cross, become visible among the Jews and Arabs who have already seen his face. Reconciliation must grow from the inside out: from Jerusalem to Judea, Samaria and the end of the world.

This means that reconciliation must first take place between Jews and Jews, then between Jews and Arabs, and finally between Arabs and Arabs both within and outside Israel. Then, according to Isaiah 19:24–25, God will form them together as an instrument for the worldwide body of Christ, an instrument which testifies to and releases reconciliation.

When they are broken in this way, according to Isaiah 57:15, the God who became flesh will himself dwell between Ishmael and his people Israel. He will display his glory among them, which will enable both of them to be a blessing in the midst of the earth.

> *"For this is what the high and lofty one says –*
>   *he who lives forever, whose name is holy:*
> *'I live in a high and holy place,*
>   *but also with him who is contrite and lowly in spirit,*
> *to revive the spirit of the lowly*
>   *and to revive the heart of the contrite.'"*
>
> (Isaiah 57:15)

From the humility which heals this oldest of wounds and divisions, a new kind of healing and reconciliation power can be born. This will not only create healing and reconciliation for the body of Christ itself. It can also release and enable Christ's body to carry reconciliation and healing with new authority out into the world.

Therefore, from my understanding of God's Word, reconciliation between Jews and Arabs should be one of our highest priorities. This must go along with leading the Jewish people to its Messiah Jesus (*Yeshua*), the restoration of Israel and the proclamation of the Gospel among Ishmael's descendants. It is for the body of messianic Jews, for the Arab churches and for the body of Christ as a whole.

The promise includes Egypt

Some may wonder why Isaiah 19 indicates that Egypt, along with Ishmael (Assyria) will be part of the covenant of blessing with Israel.

Egypt has a special place in God's history in many regards. Egypt was the house of slavery for Israel, and for that it was judged. But it was also a place of refuge for Abraham, Joseph, Jacob, and not least for the Messiah himself.

We should also remember that during Joseph's day, Pharaoh asked Jacob to bless him. In honoring this expression of humility, God includes Egypt in the special calling of Abraham's descendants in spite of all the judgments on that nation. This is one of the reasons that Egypt, along with Israel, is one of the few ancient peoples which continue to exist as a people and a nation – because God still intends to use Egypt in his plan of salvation.

In Isaiah 19:23 we read that there will be a highway between Egypt and Assyria (Arab peoples) and that they will develop a lively relationship with each other.

> *"In that day there will be a highway from Egypt to Assyria. The Assyrians will go to Egypt and the Egyptians to Assyria. The Egyptians and Assyrians will worship together."*

What can this mean? A possible and even plausible explanation is that just as Abraham is Ishmael's father, the Egyptian Hagar is his mother. God created the child–parent relationship in such a way that it is the mother who encourages, promotes and watches over the child's first steps in life and his approach to the father.

It could also be in the future that Egypt (Hagar) could play a motherly role toward Ishmael (the Arabs) by going ahead of the Arab peoples in reconciliation with the Jewish people. Egypt could take them by the hand and lead them back into the father's house of faith and to their brother Isaac.

Didn't Sadat do just that politically in 1973 by courageously going ahead of all the Arabs to Jerusalem, thus demonstrating that peace with Israel is possible? He paid for it with his life because reconciliation always has a price. But his deed showed something central to his people's calling.

Happily, there are individual Egyptians who impressively live their people's calling in relationship to the Jewish people. But I wish that more Egyptian Christians could understand Sadat's prophetic deed and have his courage to lead their people into their calling. This would certainly bring with it the liberation of Egypt from the yoke of Islam.

Egypt *will* enter its calling. The only question is how much suffering and misery must be caused by the present opposition to God's plans. Is it not astonishing that these very peoples who are destined to be a center of blessing together are known to the whole contemporary world? Is it not strange that, though still in a negative way, they are in everyone's mouth?

Rebellion against God instead of trust

God is preparing to fulfill his promises and plans. Yet our world's rebellion against the biblical God has resulted in the enmity, violence and darkness which characterize present relations among these peoples.

How tragic that this has centered in Jerusalem, which Jesus called the city of the great king, in other words, the Messiah. Jerusalem, the city of peace and salvation, has become a city of horror, of terror, of irreconcilable contradictions and of hatred.

This rebellion is rooted in a deep mistrust of God. It neither understands nor believes that his goal is the salvation of all peoples.

Isaiah 2:3–4 commands God's people,

> *"Come, let us go up to the mountain of the* LORD,
> *to the house of the God of Jacob.*
> *He will teach us his ways,*
> *so that we may walk in his paths.*
> *The law will go out from Zion,*
> *the word of the* LORD *from Jerusalem.*
> *He will judge between the nations*
> *and will settle disputes for many peoples.*
> *They will beat their swords into plowshares . . .*
> *Nation will not take up sword against nation . . . "*

God's strategy

God has chosen the only strategy that can bring salvation. All pride must break under this strategy, because it is for God himself incredibly humiliating. He chose a stiff-necked, proud, ungrateful people and bound his name to them for all time as *"the God of Israel."*

He placed himself and his name in their hands, revealed himself to them, showed them his glory, and set up his tabernacle among them. He endured their endless misuse and desecration of his name. Although he disciplined them with harsh judgments and scattered them among all the peoples, he never forsook them, never rejected them, never cancelled his plans to make them his witnesses and a light to the nations (Isaiah 43:10 and 44:8).

In the incarnation of the Messiah, the only Son of the Father, he even became part of this people. Isaiah 9:6,

> *"For to us a child is born,*
> *to us a son is given,*
> *and the government will be on his shoulders.*

And he will be called
> Wonderful Counselor, Mighty God,
> Everlasting Father, Prince of Peace."

John 1:18 says,

> "No one has ever seen God, but God the only Son, who is at the Father's side, has made him known."

Jesus became a curse in order to take on himself all of creation's darkness and destroy it on the cross. Through the conquest of death and through the resurrection, light, grace, and truth broke forth and were borne by this chosen people to all the nations, as the prophet Jeremiah promised,

> "... to you the nations will come ... and say,
> 'Our fathers possessed nothing but false gods...'"
>   (Jeremiah 16:19)

Thus Isaiah 25:6–8 will also be fulfilled:

> "On this mountain the LORD Almighty will prepare
>   a feast of rich food for all peoples...
> On this mountain he will destroy
>   the shroud that enfolds all peoples,
> the sheet that covers all nations;
>   he will swallow up death forever.
> The Sovereign LORD will wipe away the tears
>   from all faces;
> he will remove the disgrace of his people [Israel]
>   from all the earth."

Zechariah 8:23 too will be fulfilled:

> "In those days ten men from all languages and nations will take firm hold of one Jew by the edge of his robe and say, 'Let us go with you, because we have heard that God is with you.'"

The shattering of Islam

God's strategy will break the pride of Islam and of the Arab peoples who rely on power and the sword to attain sovereignty, renown and the top positions. They call God's Word, both Old and New Testament, a forgery and a lie; they replace it with their own creed which serves their pride and their honor. The pride and power of Islam and the Arab nations must be broken for them to understand the truth of Jeremiah 16:19, *"Our fathers possessed nothing but false gods."*

Once they are liberated from the lie of Islam, they will be free to enter the promised blessing along with Israel and become a blessing for the world. The Arab peoples and Egypt can receive the promised blessing only alongside Israel. They must bow under the mighty hand of the God of Israel and humbly acknowledge that God has never rejected the Jewish people. On the contrary: Hundreds of times he promised through his prophets that after a period of judgment and scattering, he would gather them again from all nations. He will bring them to the land promised them since Abraham.

In order for the Arab and Egyptian people to enter their calling, they must accept the fact that after 2,000 years God has restored the Jews as a nation in the land of Israel. There he will use them as a vessel and as messengers of his end-time salvation.

"Salvation is from the Jews" (John 4:22) will one day be confessed by Ishmael's descendants, for the Messiah they will acknowledge and to whom they will pay homage is a Jewish Messiah and king.

He was born a Jewish Messiah and king, died a Jewish Messiah and king, and will return a Jewish Messiah and king in order to reign over a Jerusalem which is the capital of the Jewish people. For he is the light which will illumine the Jewish people and which will be carried *"to the ends of the earth."*

Israel must humble itself

"God opposes the proud but gives grace to the humble" (1 Peter 5:5).
Every form of pride will be shattered on the humility of Israel's
God.

But the pride of the Jewish people must also be shattered
through God's strategy. Israel must learn that it cannot acquire
the Promised Land, the land of the fathers, by its own abilities,
strength or religious achievements.

Israel has neither the right to grasp the land for itself nor
the right to give it away, because it is God's land, on which the
eyes of God rest (Deuteronomy 11:10–14). God gives it to
Israel as a gift, as a dowry, as a place to meet him. Not by
might nor by power, but by the Spirit of God will land and
people be restored (Zechariah 4:6). Jewish humanism, Jewish
religiosity, Jewish intellect, the Israeli army must bow and
confess, *"Unless the* LORD *builds the house, its builders labor in
vain"* (Psalm 127:1).

Israel will learn that neither she nor her mighty allies are
able to create and guarantee peace and security in this land.
They can only turn and cry out to the one who is able to bring
peace to this land because it is *his* land. He is the root and the
branch of David, the One who says of himself, *"I am the way
and the truth and the life. No one comes to the Father except through
me"* (John 14:6).

When he intervenes he will neither take sides nor heed
historic rights and national pride. He will create life, peace, and
freedom for all – but only on his conditions.

The pride of the nations

But the pride of the nations will also be broken through God's
strategy. In Psalm 2 we read that the mighty of the world will
revolt against the God of Israel and his Messiah.

God stretches out his hand against these mighty ones through the very people they have hated, despised, rejected, persecuted and killed throughout the centuries. Israel, which had epitomized rejection and been called the leper and refuse of the world, becomes the messenger of good news and of life, as the servant of the Almighty.

Receiving and honoring Israel as the one who shows the way to him who is the light of the world will deflate the pride of the nations. The nations will have to cry out, *"Let us go with you, because we have heard that God is with you"* (Zechariah 8:23).

The nations will learn to love and honor Israel, just as Israel learns to love and honor Jesus – whom it had hated, despised, and persecuted – when it recognizes him as the "one who was pierced."

The Church

The pride of the Church must also be shattered through God's strategy. How often has the Church misunderstood God, thinking that he had given up or disinherited the Jewish people, that he removed their purpose or even destined them to judgment! As if God were fickle and unreliable in his promises and callings! *"For God's gifts and his call are irrevocable!"* (Romans 11:29).

If Israel had not been called, there would not be a Church; if Israel is not restored and released for its calling, the great harvest of God's kingdom will not be brought in (Zechariah 8:23; Isaiah 14). The Church is called to partake in the calling of the Jewish people, but it cannot replace them.

According to Ephesians 2:19 the Church is a fellow citizen and participant, rather than the sole possessor of God's salvation and calling. The Church's fruitfulness depends on its unity and bond with the older, first-called and first-born brother.

The Church must again confess before the world, "My Lord and Messiah Jesus is the king of the Jews, and the Jews are my people. We as a Church belong to them; their life and their history affect us directly."

Like Ruth in the Bible, the Church will have to confess, *"Where you go I will go, and where you stay I will stay. Your people will be my people and your God my God"* (Ruth 1:16). If the Church is unwilling to stand by the Jewish people and share the slander, the persecutions and the hatred which they still encounter, then it will likewise not be able to share the fruitfulness, power and authority which God promised Israel.

Like Paul we could say that all the authority which the Church has so far experienced is nothing compared to what will be when God has released Israel into its calling (see Romans 11:15). The Church must humble itself under God's mighty hand so that he can raise it up again at his time and on his conditions (1 Peter 5:6).

When the Church confesses that its Messiah Jesus is the king of the Jews and that the Jewish people is its people, it will become an outsider and will itself be despised, persecuted, and hated. But that is the path to the fullness of the inheritance.

The whole world is affected

The Near East conflict affects not only Arabs and Jews, but the whole world. For the restoration of Israel is not the result of human, but of divine work – even if God uses men and institutions, e.g. the UNO in 1948. Much suffering is caused by the fact that his work, whose goal is the salvation of the world, is so strongly opposed by the Jewish people, by the non-Jewish world, and by the Church.

God's work with and in Israel reveals the heart attitude of both the Jewish people and the rest of the world toward himself and his Word. Every person will be compelled sooner or later to decide: Is my standard and authority the word of the Bible or my own human, religious or secular view?

The God of the old and the new covenant offers the Jewish people and the whole world life, peace and salvation in Jesus. Refusing or opposing this offer has its consequences. If the biblical God alone is life and love – and he is! – then a life without him can end only in suffering, misery and death.

Chapter 5

Israel – a Light to the Peoples

Jesus instructed his disciples to stand by his people, to love them and through our life and friendship bring them the hope which became flesh in the Jewish Messiah Jesus. This is the promised hope of which the prophets speak.

> " 'The time is coming,' declares the LORD,
>   'when I will make a new covenant
> with the house of Israel
>   and with the house of Judah.
> It will not be like the covenant
>   I made with their forefathers
> when I took them by the hand
>   to lead them out of Egypt,
> because they broke my covenant,
>   though I was a husband to them,'
>   declares the LORD.
> 'This is the covenant that I will make with
>   the house of Israel
>   after that time,' declares the LORD.

'I will put my law in their minds
and write it on their hearts.
I will be their God,
and they will be my people . . .
For I will forgive their wickedness
and will remember their sins no more.'"

(Jeremiah 31:31–34)

"Comfort, comfort my people,
says your God.
Speak tenderly to Jerusalem,
and proclaim to her
that her hard service has been completed,
that her sin has been paid for."

(Isaiah 40:1–2)

That is why it is important to acquire insight into what God is doing with and through Israel.

Why was Israel chosen?

What is so mysterious and special, what is so totally unusual about the Jewish people and their history which makes them unavoidably visible, irritating and fascinating for everyone else? No other people has for thousands of years so continuously and intensively aroused others' emotions through its mere existence.

If we look for the reason we will first of all establish that the Jews as a people, as a race, and as persons are just as good and just as bad as other peoples, races, and persons.

The prophet Jeremiah said regarding this,

"The heart is deceitful above all things
and beyond cure."

(Jeremiah 17:9)

And Paul quotes,

> *"There is no-one righteous, not even one;*
> *there is no-one who understands,*
> *no-one who seeks God.*
> *All have turned away,*
> *they have together become worthless;*
> *there is no-one who does good,*
> *not even one."*

(Romans 3:10–12)

This is true for all people, whether Jew or non-Jew. In make-up and quality there is no difference.

Then what makes this people so prominent? Why the explicit bond between God and Israel's history, which keeps provoking one of two reactions: either sympathy, love, respect, even idolization – or hate, contempt, persecution and destruction?

God woos peoples

The mystery lies in the relationship which the Creator of heaven and earth has to Israel. He has revealed himself as *"the God of Israel."* The history of Israel, the Jewish people, is a history of God's striving, suffering, hoping, even wooing of the earth's peoples. In and through Israel, God woos all peoples to turn to him in order to be saved.

Abraham's calling already had this clear goal:

> *"I will make you into a great nation*
> *and I will bless you;*
> *I will make your name great,*
> *and you will be a blessing.*
> *I will bless those who bless you,*
> *and whoever curses you I will curse,*

and all peoples on earth
   will be blessed through you."

(Genesis 12:2–3)

This promise would be conclusively fulfilled in the Messiah Jesus, who became flesh. Through the people who were his brothers, the blessing and God's care was to flow to the peoples. *"All will be blessed through you . . . "*

God's goal both for his people and for all other peoples is that they be free from death once and for all. He wants to give them full life on Mount Zion and bring all peoples into the eternal feast and eternal joy.

"On this mountain the LORD Almighty will prepare
   a feast of rich food for all peoples . . .
On this mountain he will destroy
   the shroud that enfolds all peoples,
the sheet that covers all nations;
   he will swallow up death for ever.
The Sovereign LORD will wipe away the tears
   from all faces;
he will remove the disgrace of his people
   from all the earth."

(Isaiah 25:6–8)

Mount Zion is not only the Mount Zion in Jerusalem or the city of Jerusalem as a whole. "Mount Zion" stands for God's intimate relationship to his people. It is a relationship which will one day save, heal and change the heart of his people and with them the hearts of all peoples.

Everyone who places himself under the Messiah Jesus' Lordship will thus become a citizen of his kingdom. Yes, they will even become a member of his family.

God's presence is the condition for life

In order to understand Israel's election we must go back to the beginnings of God's history with creation, specifically with man.

> *"In the beginning God created the heavens and the earth. Now the earth was formless and empty, darkness was over the surface of the deep."*
>
> (Genesis 1:1–2)

The earth had neither life and nor the possibility of life.

> *"And God said, 'Let there be light' and there was light."*
>
> (Genesis 1:3)

This was not the creation of the sun and moon, which is reported later. The light spoken of here is God's presence, his being and reality. This is the condition for every form of life and growth, all the more for relationship and fellowship. Therefore the Messiah Jesus, who is the essence of God's reality and presence, said later, *"I am the light of the world"* (John 8:12).

John declared, regarding peoples' relationships and fellowship among themselves,

> *"But if we walk in the light, as he is in the light, we have fellowship with one another, and the blood of Jesus, his Son, purifies us from all sin."*
>
> (1 John 1:7)

To walk in the light means nothing other than to consciously live in God's presence.

Into this revelation of his presence, God created man in order to have fellowship with him. God entrusted the creation to man, who – in fellowship with God – would lead it into the fullness of life. The creation was to unfold its full bloom and fruitfulness in the presence of man living in and from fellowship with God.

Life in darkness

Instead of that, the immense, incomprehensible and death-bringing tragedy came through man. His severed relationship, resulting from disobedience and rebellion, caused him to fall out of God's presence and thus out of fellowship with God. But without fellowship with God, man can have no life-bringing fellowship with his neighbor, either. After falling out of God's light, man found himself back in darkness, in a desolate, formless, and empty world.

> *"See, darkness covers the earth*
> *and thick darkness is over the peoples."*
>
> (Isaiah 60:2)

This was the situation of the earth and its inhabitants once again. Paul says it even more clearly. *"Their foolish hearts were darkened"* (Romans 1:21).

In this darkness, that is, no longer living in God's presence, all life dies. God predicted this, not as a threat or punishment, but simply as a consequence.

> *"... when you eat of* [the tree of the knowledge of good and evil] *you will surely die."*
>
> (Genesis 2:17)

The first thing people realized was that they were naked. The reality of nakedness, fear, and abandonment destroys life. Death reigns.

When the Bible speaks of nakedness and shame it means not only physical nakedness, but primarily inner bareness. The person is ashamed of the loss of his dignity and value, which are his only in relationship and fellowship with the Creator and King of the universe. Therefore, inferiority feelings and loss of value influence the perception and behavior of everyone on earth.

Nakedness is the loss of identity. I no longer know where I came from, where I'm going, or why I exist. If I no longer know who my Creator is, I don't know who I am either, rendering any healthy relationship to myself impossible.

Besides inferiority feelings and loss of identity, darkness also brings fear. Fear means no longer knowing who God is, what God is like, and what he is like with me. A person who does not know God and has no access to him is defenselessly abandoned to evil powers and to circumstances.

"Darkness covers the earth and thick darkness is over the peoples..." Men no longer know who God is; they are given over to death because they live under the reign of darkness. The only alternative to fellowship with God and obedience to him is death, cold and darkness.

Back to the Promised Land

However, God did not give up his creation because he, the Creator of heaven and earth, is love in person.

> *"For God so loved the world that he gave his one and only Son, that whoever believes in him shall not perish but have eternal life."*
> (John 3:16).

> *"I take no pleasure in the death of the wicked, but rather that they turn from their ways and live. Turn! Turn from your evil ways! Why will you die, O house of Israel?"*
> (Ezekiel 33:11)

God takes no pleasure in the death of the person who is ruled by darkness.

In this darkness God looked for a person who would enable him to reveal himself, who would care for his creation again and reveal him again to all peoples. Abraham qualified as this person after God's heart because of his unconditional will to have fellowship with and be obedient to God. This is impressively demonstrated in his willingness to sacrifice Isaac.

Under God's guidance Abraham, who was not yet a Jew but according to his own testimony an Aramean, became a *Hebrew*, i.e. one who crosses over. He crossed over from the reign of darkness to the land of promise, where God rules.

Abraham and his descendants from Jacob became channels of blessing and of God's care for the peoples. *"All peoples will be blessed through you"* (Genesis 12:3). In them God's presence, his reality, and his being were revealed.

God decided, as he had promised Abraham, to show the peoples that he was the living, holy, true, just, but also the loving and merciful God. He demonstrated this in the way he dealt with Abraham and his descendants. Through Israel God calls to the nations,

> *"Though your sins are like scarlet,*
> *they shall be as white as snow."*

(Isaiah 1:18)

God's people

As we have already said, Israel as a people is morally and ethically no better than any others. Only God's work and the presence of the Holy Spirit have made Israel a holy people; this has separated Israel from all other peoples, who are living under the reign of darkness.

Israel is a people visibly different from all others, unique in its history and its faith. We must not forget that the powers of darkness and death controlled the peoples all around Israel. These powers demanded worship and service, expressed in human sacrifice, licentiousness, and perversion.

It was solely God's relationship to Israel which made Israel different from all other peoples. Israel's election, the prominence, separation, and sanctification of this people are not a question of merit or special character, as often thought. It is due simply to the fact that the sole living and true God revealed himself to Israel and bound his name once and for all with them. He wanted to reveal himself to his creation once again as the God of this people.

As Creator, God wants to demonstrate his fatherhood in Israel so that all nations will see it and begin longing for him. Israel is the place of God's revelation in this world.

All the nations need to know that there is no God like the God of Israel, who loves, protects, and cares. He is the one who frees his people from distress and misery, protecting them like the apple of his eye, but who is also a Father who instructs, punishes, and puts in order, who forgives and restores.

There is no God like the God of Israel who strives for his people and takes responsibility for them, who has thoughts of salvation and peace for them. Israel is to be a witness that there is no other God than the living God, the creator of heaven and earth.

Israel: where God reveals himself

This knowledge that the God of Israel is different from all other gods gradually penetrates the darkness and lights up the hearts of individual persons and peoples. For example, the Hittites recognized that Abraham was a prince of God and had a special relationship to the living God (Genesis 23:6 and following).

Genesis 26:27 and elsewhere testifies of Isaac that God is obviously with him as with no other.

In Exodus 18:11 the Midianite Jethro exclaimed admiringly and worshipfully, *"Now I know that the Lord is greater than all other gods"* because he was overwhelmed by God's dealings with Israel.

Later the prostitute Rahab, who took in the spies, declared that no one can withstand the God of Israel because he is different from all other gods (Joshua 2:11). The queen of Sheba recognized God's character in the way he dealt with Israel.

> *"Praise be to the LORD your God, who has delighted in you."*
> (1 Kings 10:9)

What a testimony from the mouths of those who lived in fear of their gods! During the course of further centuries God continued to reveal himself. For example, the Babylonian Nebuchadnezzar had to confess before Daniel, *"Your God is truly the God of gods"* (Daniel 2:47). The testimony continued. God had begun to penetrate the darkness of the peoples through his history with Israel.

Israel is a witness

But Israel is not only the place where God reveals himself. Israel itself should also witness to this revelation.

> *"You are my witnesses,"* declares the LORD,
> *"and my servant whom I have chosen,*
> *so that you may know and believe me*
> *and understand that I am he.*
> *Before me no god was formed,*
> *nor will there be one after me."*
>
> (Isaiah 43:10)

In Isaiah 44:8, God repeats this,

> *"You are my witnesses. Is there any God besides me?*
>   *No, there is no other Rock; I know not one."*

It is not because Israel is stronger or better than others that they come and fall down before him, but because God dwells with him.

> *"This is what the LORD says:*
>
> *'The products of Egypt and the merchandise of Cush,*
>   *and those tall Sabeans –*
> *they will come over to you*
>   *and will be yours;*
> *they will trudge behind you,*
>   *coming over to you in chains.*
> *They will bow before you*
>   *and plead with you, saying,*
> *"Surely God is with you, and there is no other;*
>   *there is no other god." '*
> *Truly you are a God who hides himself,*
>   *O God and Savior of Israel."*
>
> (Isaiah 45:14–15)

God repeatedly challenges Israel not to keep this revelation to themselves but to carry it to the nations. One day it will even come to the point where ten men from all languages and nations will grasp the hem of one Jew's garment, saying, *"Let us go with you, because we have heard that God is with you"* (Zechariah 8:23).

The nation of Israel is the place of God's revelation; the people's calling is to testify to him among the nations.

Chapter 6

The Messiah and the Land

In the Near East conflict there is no issue more controversial, more emotional or more provocative than the question of the land.

To whom does the land belong? Who possesses how much land? What is Israel, what is Palestine? Is the name Palestine even justified? Until this name was introduced by the Romans under Caesar Hadrian around AD 135 it had been known only as Israel. These are the misgivings of some.

For some it is a matter of Christian love and justice to make a Palestinian state from the so-called occupied territories as soon as possible. This area, known as Judea and Samaria in the Bible, is considered Israel's biblical heartland.

Hebron, a city of 120,000, is the place alongside Jerusalem with the deepest Jewish roots and the greatest Jewish identity. Here Abraham lived; here he and Sarah were buried. David, with whom the kingdom of Israel was really inaugurated, reigned his first seven years in Hebron.

Today this city is in Islamic–Arabic hands; the small Jewish group living there is seen worldwide as a source of conflict which must be obliterated. Not only Muslims and a substantial number of Christians agree with this, but also a significant number of Jews who want peace at any price.

When we turn to Jerusalem, agonizingly irreconcilable concepts and claims clash all the more. Facts and history are insufficient to deal adequately with Jerusalem. It cannot be understood with human intellect alone.

Jesus himself lifted Jerusalem above the mundane and profane when he forbade swearing by it, *"because it is the city of the great king"* (Matthew 5:35). In other words, Jerusalem is the city of the Messiah, Jesus' own city.

Today Jerusalem has become the immovable stone cited by the prophet Zechariah (12:3): *"All who try to move it will injure themselves."*

Does "Christian Zionism" hinder the fulfillment of the missionary commission?

Many committed Christians ask themselves whether the controversy over Israel as a people and a country, over Jerusalem and Hebron, is not simply a side track or even a false path which distracts us from our real task – which is to take the Gospel to the nations and make disciples.

Some argue that if we wish to win Muslims for Jesus, we cannot afford to provoke them with "Christian Zionism." It is a stumbling block not only for Muslims, but also for many non-Muslims, because it testifies that the Old Testament land promises to Israel are still valid and that God is bringing the Jewish people back to the land promised them. Therefore it is understandable when every effort is made to eliminate the stumbling block of "the restoration of the people and land of Israel" and when any spiritual meaning is interpreted away.

Zionism – a stumbling stone

Christian theologians are still providing rational, plausible interpretations and proofs with which to keep the stumbling block of "Zionism" at a painless distance. Some are even convinced that they are thus serving God.

It is argued that the land promises to Israel and the specific calling of Israel as a people and a nation – namely to be a kingdom of priests and witnesses to God's kingdom rule on earth, as well as a light and signpost to the nations, according to Zechariah 8:22–23 – have been fulfilled with the coming of the Messiah, in whom the Church becomes their heir.

Israel as a nation has thus lost its meaning, as we read in Shakespeare's *Othello*, "The Moor has fulfilled his duty, the Moor can go." Some generously concede a function to Israel in the thousand-year kingdom, but only after Israel as a people has been converted. Yet the conclusion is the same: At present, that is as long as the Church has not been raptured, Israel has no more meaning than any other nation.

Making the Old Testament relative

"For I will take you out of the nations; I will gather you from all the countries and bring you back into your own land."
(Ezekiel 36:24)

"Then they will know that I am the LORD their God, for though I sent them into exile among the nations, I will gather them to their own land . . .
(Ezekiel 39:28)

"See, I will bring them from the land of the north
and gather them from the ends of the earth."
(Jeremiah 31:8)

"This is what the LORD Almighty says: 'I will save my people from the countries of the east and the west. I will bring them back to live in Jerusalem . . .'"
(Zechariah 8:7–8)

This passionate promise of God to his people shines like a pillar of fire throughout their history. Yet for many Christians, the fact that Israel now exists again as a nation is merely the solution to an ethnic minority's humanitarian and political problem; the solution cannot be at the cost of another people.

This is a defective view of Israel and its actual restoration as a people and a nation. It is nourished by a theology which says that the Old Testament can be assessed only by the New Testament. In other words, we understand Israel's destiny and calling purely by the statements of Jesus and the Apostles. But since the New Testament has little to say about this, the conclusion is drawn that Israel has no further meaning for God's work of salvation.

Israel's history and God's promises to this people are spiritualized. The Old Testament is considered a book full of metaphors and images which now point only to the coming of the Messiah and the birth of the Church.

For example, Peter Walker, professor for New Testament at the University of Oxford, writes in *The Bible and the Land* (Musalaha 2000, p. 115), "The land and the Torah are only a temporary, passing stage of God's salvation history." In other words, God's promises in the Old Testament have no further meaning today because everything has been fulfilled and abrogated by the Messiah.

If the Old Testament is a document of a passing nature, it would then be consistent to view all the divine promises contained in it as merely relative to that time. Texts such as Numbers 23:19, *"God is not a man, that he should lie, nor a son of man, that he should change his mind. Does he speak and then not act?"* would lose their meaning. Likewise, Paul's statements in Romans 11:29, *"God's gifts and his call are irrevocable"* become questionable with this theology.

Yet we know God's Word is eternal and that the Lord is the same whether revealed in the Old Testament or in Jesus.

Thank God that we read of him, *"The word of the* LORD *is right and true; he is faithful in all he does"* (Psalm 33:4). Likewise we can trust that *"Here is a trustworthy saying that deserves full acceptance"* (1 Timothy 1:15; 4:9).

Romans 9–11

In Romans 9–11 Paul thoroughly illuminates the question of Israel. He draws the conclusion that God has not rejected the actual Israel. On the contrary, Israel is *"loved on account of the patriarchs"* even as an enemy of the Gospel (Romans 11:28). The promises and the covenants are still valid for this people.

When Paul says that Israel has not been rejected he does not refer to their salvation, but to their very specific calling as a people and a nation. God has not rejected Israel. That means he still has a plan for this nation.

It is true that the Church has been born and shares Israel's calling, namely to be light and salt for the world. The Church expresses this in a particular way. But what then is Israel's calling as a nation, if it is not totally identical with that of the Church?

The Church

According to 2 Corinthians 5:18, the Church is called to the *"ministry of reconciliation."* Through the Church God woos men to repentance. Through the Church he offers forgiveness and sonship, in and through the saving act of his Son, the Messiah Jesus.

During this time of grace, the Messiah knocks at our hearts' doors and waits to be let in, so that he can build a heart relationship with us. Grace means that God never forces reconciliation and repentance on anyone, neither through might nor through power – even though the Church itself has seldom understood this or acted accordingly.

Not by coincidence is it said of the Messiah, *"A bruised reed he will not break, and a smoldering wick he will not snuff out"* (Matthew 12:20 and Isaiah 42:3). A person's repentance, his "yes" to God's love offered in his Son can be attained only in total freedom of choice. This is not only a matter of being saved from hell, but of entering a *relationship of love*.

That is why we speak of the Bride, who is formed from Jews and non-Jews; from the first-fruits of Jews and heathen. Therefore the Church's message is universal but personal. It calls the individuals out of all natural bonds; their "yes" to Jesus' act of salvation and their own love for Jesus render them part of the Bride.

Love and anger

God became man in order to expose evil in every form of human existence; to judge it and dispose of it.

> *"The reason the Son of God appeared was to destroy the devil's work."*
>
> (1 John 3:8)

Overcoming evil in the life of an individual is one thing. And yet it is a fact that even though *"light has come into the world . . . men loved darkness instead of light because their deeds were evil"* (John 3:19).

Now that God has overcome evil (Colossians 2:14–15) through his suffering (Isaiah 53), will he allow the enemy to continue to rage unbounded? Remember that this enemy through pride, arrogance and rebellion against God deludes and rules mankind and thus all of creation, driving them into ruin.

If God's wrath against evil has not yet been fully revealed – thus leading many to consider him powerless, weak, and irrelevant – this is solely because *"he is patient with you, not wanting anyone to perish"* (1 Peter 3:9). He *"takes no pleasure in the death of the wicked, but rather that they may turn from their ways and live"* (Ezekiel 33:11).

It is difficult for us to speak of God's wrath, even though it is often mentioned in the New Testament, e.g. John 3:36,

> *"Whoever rejects the Son will not see life, for God's wrath remains on him."*

In his parables, Jesus speaks not only about the Father's love, but also about the wrath of the king who throws his rebellious and unfaithful servants into darkness or has them cut apart, in order to eliminate evil (Matthew 18:34; 24:51; 25:30). We Christians have often cultivated a much too humanistic standard with which to judge God according to human needs and concepts. This puts us in danger of amalgamating with the world and calling God to account, instead of ourselves and others being called to account by God's Word.

It is difficult for us to reconcile this characteristic of God, who is angry over evil in men, who calls to account and judges, with the picture of Jesus as the good shepherd. Because of this, many Christians have problems with the Old Testament and with the history of Israel.

For example, more and more Christians now speak about the land conquest under Joshua as "unacceptable ethnic cleansing." We suppress the fact that God not only gathers people for the wedding feast from the highways and byways, but also throws out into the darkness the guest who entered without wedding clothes, i.e. without fulfilling the host's conditions.

As much as God is endlessly merciful, forgiving and loving, so he is also the one who will reign with an iron scepter over arrogant and rebellious peoples; he will break pride and rebellion just as one breaks earthly jars (Psalm 2; Revelation 2:27; 12:5; 19:15–16).

Judgment on the nations

Through the Church the Messiah stretches out his forgiving hand to the rebellious nations (Acts 4:27–31). But at the end of the age he will come through Israel to judge them so that they experience the consequences of their rebellion and learn justice.

> *"When your judgments come upon the earth,*
>   *the people of the world learn righteousness."*
>
> (Isaiah 26:9)

It is difficult for us to see this trait of God's because it is not harmless; it confronts us with judgment and the repercussions of pride and rebellion. In Psalm 2 we read, *"I have installed my King on Zion"* and the nations must bow under his reign.

There will be no more coaxing and wooing, only God's claim to sovereignty. He will appear in his power in order to break pride and rebellion which as an embodiment of evil are a source of darkness, destruction and death for his creation. God will conclusively break and eliminate evil; everything which refuses salvation through this judgment will be annihilated along with it.

This will be the time of which we read,

> *"They called to the mountains and the rocks, 'Fall on us and hide us from the face of him who sits on the throne and from the wrath of the Lamb! For the great day of their wrath has come, and who can stand?' "*
>
> (Revelation 6:16–17)

This will pertain to Israel as well as to the nations (Zephaniah 3:11–15). Israel will also be purged of its pride and arrogance until it is a godly, humble people trusting in God alone.

The return of the Jewish people to Israel and their restoration as a nation in the land promised them will begin to birth the incarnation of God's reign over all nations. Through his people the Jews, and through his land, Israel, God will summon the peoples of the earth in order to call them to account and demand obedience to his Word.

When the nations are confronted with God's sovereignty through Israel, it will be revealed who submits to the Lord of the whole earth, and who rebels against him. The Lamb of God, whose kingdom was not of this world, appears as the Lion from the tribe of Judah who will reign in this world.

"In the last days

the mountain of the LORD's temple will be established
    as chief among the mountains;
it will be raised above the hills,
    and all nations will stream to it.

Many peoples will come and say,

'Come, let us go up to the mountain of the LORD,
    to the house of the God of Jacob.
He will teach us his ways,
    so that we may walk in his paths.'
The law will go out from Zion,
    the word of the LORD from Jerusalem.
He will judge between the nations
    and will settle disputes for many peoples."

(Isaiah 2:2–4)

What is Zionism?

"The law will go out from Zion." Is God a Zionist? This question may seem outlandish to many Christians. But is it so unjustified?

I realize that the term "Zionism" can be understood in many different ways. In the gamut between the purely national and the purely spiritual, there are many shades and opinions. For a time, the nations equated the term "Zionism" with "racism." Even though that was officially corrected, most people, including some Christians, associate this term with negative feelings and concepts.

Assuming that the Old Testament is truly God's Word, we can see that the term "Zionism" is derived from the biblical Zion. Zion designates a tangible place on earth, namely a mountain in Jerusalem. Mount Moriah is there, where Abraham made an altar to sacrifice Isaac and where Solomon built the temple.

For Jews, the temple with its holy of holies was and still is the quintessence of God's presence among his people. God said at its dedication,

> *"...I have consecrated this temple ... by putting my Name there forever. My eyes and my heart will always be there."*
>
> (1 Kings 9:3)

This makes Zion an appellation for God's covenant and for his relationship to his people.

Since Zion is the quintessence of God's dwelling among his people, the Bible often equates Zion and Jerusalem. But not only that; sometimes the term Zion is applied to the Jews as a people, namely when they live under God's reign in the land he has given them. In this way the people itself becomes God's dwelling.

Therefore, from a biblical standpoint the restoration of Zion is always the restoration of people and land, of the land through the people, and of filling the people and the land with God's presence. The extent to which God sees land and people together as an expression of his reign and his covenant is described in Isaiah 62:1–7.

There we read that God will marry the people and the land to each other. God names people and land *"my delight is in her"* and *"married"* (verse 4). God's will is unfolded as his people are brought together because this is the condition for making his glory and reign visible among all nations.

The Old Testament often mentions what God says about Zion. In Zechariah 8:1–5 God promises to return to Zion and fill Jerusalem again with his people, after he had turned away in judgment from the people of Israel for a time; he had scattered them and the land was desolate. God says that he himself will be zealous to restore Jerusalem and his people Israel in Zion – in wrath against everything which opposes this restoration.

God – a Zionist?

In Psalm 9:11 we read that God is *"enthroned in Zion"*; in Psalm 132:13–18 God says he will dwell in Zion forever in order to bring salvation to his people from there. Psalm 146:10, Psalm 2:6 and Joel 2:1 speak of Zion as the dwelling of the most high, his holy mountain. And, as quoted above, *"The law will go out from Zion, the word of the LORD from Jerusalem."*

The nations will go up to Jerusalem (Zion) to worship and to pay homage to the Messiah. He will proclaim justice and bring them peace. (See Micah 4:7, Zechariah 14:16 and Isaiah 2:2–4.)

Yes, God is truly *the* Zionist. He will restore Zion by restoring the people and land of Israel; he himself will dwell among this people in this land. Then justice, orientation, instruction, help and salvation will go out from Zion to all peoples of the earth. This will no longer be a matter of individuals only, but of the nations (Micah 4 and Isaiah 2).

Whoever opposes God's Zionistic plans is opposing not simply the Jews or the state of Israel or the "impossible" settlers; he is opposing the goal of divine Zionism, namely to release salvation, justice and peace for the nations. But this will not take place without the restoration of the old covenant people. Since God keeps his word, the restoration of Zion is an absolute necessity for the sake of his honor, but also for the sake of the nations. God is a Zionist and every person who is concerned for the salvation of the nations should join him as quickly as possible!

Many find it very difficult to believe that one day the Messiah's reign on this earth will be manifested through the Jewish people, of all things. As if it weren't enough that the Messiah is to reign as God–King from a concrete piece of earth, namely from Israel, with Jerusalem as its capital! This is more-over going to take place through a specific people who are his officials and servants (priests and heralds), namely the Jewish people.

Controversial Israel

The perceptions and faith of Jewish prophets, apostles and scholars have influenced nearly half of current mankind in one way or another. The Messiah himself became flesh in this people. Nevertheless, no other people makes the nations' blood boil to the extent that the Jewish people does; they are either idolized or hated. Their behavior is deemed proud, obstinate and inconsiderate, absolutely unsuitable for servants in God's kingdom, which is said to be holy, just and true.

At present, such an idea is even more difficult to compre-hend because Israel has become a center of conflict. Violent squatters, incorrigible racists, obstinate discussion partners –

this is how the world sees Israel and this is how the media present it. No reference point, no sign, no basis for the formation of the Messiah's kingdom!

Perhaps the most irritating thing for many is the fact that this people still exists – despite millennia filled with waves of annihilation and persecution. With regard to the calling of the Jewish people, one could say the same as Isaiah wrote concerning the incarnation of the Messiah, *"Who has believed our message and to whom has the arm of the LORD been revealed?"* (Isaiah 53:1).

The Jewish peoples' suffering, the way they were rejected and held in contempt remind us of the Messiah as he is described in Isaiah 53. Even though, unlike the Messiah, the Jewish people's own guilt has contributed to its suffering, it must also unwillingly bear much of the nations' guilt.

Just as the incarnation of the Messiah was not believed and accepted because it did not correspond to human expectations, so the incarnation of the coming kingdom of the "Lion of Judah" will not be believed and accepted until the iron scepter lies on the necks of the nations.

"Blessed are those who have not seen and yet have believed."
(John 20:29)

The test of faithfulness

I often have the impression that, unlike Moses, the Church has not passed the test of faithfulness. God made Moses the offer that he would let the people of Israel fall because of their unfaithfulness, in order to begin something new with Moses and make a new chosen people with him. Moses vehemently resisted this. Why?

Moses did not want God to seem a failure in the eyes of the nations!

*"Why should the Egyptians say, 'It was with evil intent that he
brought them out, to kill them in the mountains?' "*

(Exodus 32:12)

God's honor was more important to Moses than his personal
successful future. What couldn't Moses have spared himself
in toil, trouble and suffering if he had accepted God's offer!
Moses' concern for God's honor made him a friend of God, one
who, like Abraham, was fully trusted by God.

God has never made the Church such an offer; he never said
he was finished with his old covenant people. But the Church
hastened to explain and prove in every conceivable way that
God has given up his plan with the Jewish people. It did not
matter to the Church, as it had to Moses, that God might be
seen as one who could not complete what he had begun; that
his honor, faithfulness and reliability could be damaged in the
eyes of the nations.

*"Not for the people's sake, but for your sake, my God, so
that the nations will know that you are a holy, absolutely
trustworthy and faithful God, when before their eyes you
reach the goal which glorifies and honors you, through
the restoration of your old covenant people to you!"*

(after Ezekiel 36:22–23)

God is able to transform the Jewish people – so troublesome in
the world's eyes – into light, salvation and hope for the world,
because he has planned it. God will restore Zion, in spite of all
theological, political and human rights' resistance, so that his
promise can be fulfilled.

How God desires his Church to have a Moses attitude
toward his old covenant people, the Jews, and toward his goal
with this people – for the sake of his honor!

Chapter 7

Is it "Harvest Time" in Israel?

What was sown?

When we speak of harvest time, it is difficult to hear the word "harvest" with Jewish ears. A harvest is "bringing in something". If we speak of a harvest, we must ask ourselves what was sown. Without sowing one cannot harvest.

These can be quite difficult and embarrassing questions. What was actually sown in the Jewish people, which would justify a harvest? What should be sown and what should be harvested?

What do Israel's friends want?

It is very important for us believers to ask ourselves why our relationship to this people is important. What do we seek when we come to Israel? Some come because of a guilty conscience or an awareness of history. Much has to be made good and that is a legitimate reason to come, but it cannot be the whole reason.

Other motives are more problematic. Many come here and use Israel to further their own dreams and plans for salvation.

Israel becomes a surface on which many religious needs are fulfilled. There is a desire to be part of Israel's aura as a chosen people, the mystery of the special history and God's special relationship to this people – and it really is a mystery!

But then the search for a relationship to this people is less for their sake than for the sake of my expectation of salvation. We must examine our relationship to the Jewish people. What are our motives? Why do I seek this relationship, what is my concern? What do I really want to sow?

"Comfort, comfort my people"

In view of our calling, I want to consider Isaiah 40:1–2:

> *"Comfort, comfort my people,*
> *says your God.*
> *Speak tenderly to Jerusalem,*
> *and proclaim to her*
> *that her hard service has been completed,*
> *that her sin has been paid for."*

The comfort we see here in God's Word, which we are to speak to Israel, is not cheap. It will cost our lives.

With a few exceptions, the Church has failed during the centuries to comfort the Jews in this way. The result is that the heart of the Jewish people was endlessly wounded by all the humiliation and injuries.

The face of the one in whose name the Church has spoken has become terribly distorted for the Jewish people. For them the name *Yeshua* became the quintessence of death, humiliation and violence. This was sown among the Jews for centuries! Can we now suddenly expect a harvest from nowhere? What sort of harvest would that be?

Israel's calling: a heart relationship to the Father

I am convinced that the Jewish people can find its true calling only through the Messiah. God has called Israel to be a light for the nations. How is that possible?

God called Israel to sonship, to a very personal relationship with him.

> *"I myself said,*
>
> *'How gladly would I treat you like sons*
> *and give you a desirable land,*
> *the most beautiful inheritance of any nation.'*
> *I thought you would call me 'Father'*
> *and not turn away from following me."*
>
> (Jeremiah 3:19)

Israel is called to demonstrate to the nations that God is a Father. Therefore the prophet Isaiah says,

> *"But you are our Father,*
> *though Abraham does not know us*
> *or Israel acknowledge us;*
> *you, O Lord, are our Father,*
> *our Redeemer from of old is your name."*
>
> (Isaiah 63:16)

The message which the prophets proclaimed through suffering to this people is that Israel will not experience his calling until God is his Father and he enters this most personal Father–son relationship. That is the essence of Jeremiah 31:33 and 34,

> *"I will put my law in their minds*
> *and write it on their hearts.*

I will be their God
   and they will be my people.
No longer will a man teach his neighbor,
   or a man his brother, saying 'Know the Lord,*'*
because they will all know me,
   from the least of them to the greatest."

In other words, God says, "Because I have a heart relationship to this people and I forgive their guilt, they will be my people." The question of guilt is linked to the discovery of God's fatherhood, as in Isaiah 40, "Comfort, comfort my people. Tell him that his guilt is forgiven and his hard service is completed."

Israel is called to such a heart-to-heart relationship with the Father. In the Old Testament God is called Father 15–20 times, in the New Testament over 200 times. What does Jesus say to the disciples when they ask him, *"How should we pray?"* In other words, how should we express our relationship to God?

Jesus wasn't speaking to Europeans and Americans, but to Jews. What took place was thoroughly Jewish. It was Jews who asked him and he answered Jews. There was no Christianity then. Jesus instructed his Jewish disciples, *"This is how you should pray: 'Our Father in heaven . . . ' "* (Matthew 6:9).

What is written in the New Testament is thoroughly Jewish because it was proclaimed to Jews. The discussions between Jesus and his disciples took place among Jews! This message that God is Father and that Jesus came to reveal the Father and lead people to this Father's heart was taken away by the Church. It was removed from the people to whom it was first given.

The calling stolen . . .

Recently I received a magazine dealing with co-operation between Church and religious Jewish institutions. Various articles attack every desire to make Jesus' name known to the

Jewish people in any way at all, saying that this amounts to a "spiritual holocaust."

I can understand when the Jewish side interprets this in such a way; Jesus' countenance really has been distorted in their eyes until it can no longer be recognized. But it makes me upset, sad and angry when theologians, pastors, and bishops get up and say, "This Jesus has nothing to do with Jews and it's an affront to even bring them the Gospel."

These Christians consider the Gospel an intellectual, cultural and historical achievement of non-Jews (biblically speaking, heathen); they consider it foreign and unsuitable for Jews. In this way the Jewish people's calling to be a light to the nations is stolen from them. With this theology the Church is actually attempting to render impossible the fulfillment of the Jewish people's calling. That is liberal replacement theology.

"There is nothing more embarrassing, offensive, and reprehensible," reads one article in the magazine, "than to bring the gospel to the Jewish people." An official prohibition against evangelism to Jews is demanded, of course with an appeal to religious Jewish feelings. However, it seems that those who reject Jesus as Messiah for the Jewish people no longer understand who Jesus is. Whoever rejects him as Messiah for the Jewish people questions him as Messiah in principle.

If Jesus is not the Messiah and savior of Israel, then he isn't for the rest of the world, either. Then Christianity just becomes a religion like any other.

Jesus, the king of the Jews

But the Gospel is the good news which came to the Jewish people, of whom it is written,

> *"Rejoice greatly, O Daughter of Zion!*
> *Shout, Daughter of Jerusalem!*

See, your king comes to you,
   righteous and having salvation,
   gentle and riding on a donkey,
   on a colt, the foal of a donkey.
I will take away the chariots from Ephraim
   and the war-horses from Jerusalem,
   and the battle bow will be broken."

(Zechariah 9:9–10)

The good news is that this king is coming, this king who is the promise and the essence of this people's calling. What arrogance to say to them, "This king has nothing to do with you!"

Today nothing is so contested and resisted as bringing the name *Yeshua* to his people. It will cost the life of every person who answers this call! I do not say this lightly.

The Messiah said to his Jewish disciples and thus to all who would believe in him through them, "Look, they will lay their hands on you. It will cost you something. And if they kill you, they will even think they have done a good work for God."

This is not an exaggerated appeal, motivated by end-time emotions and a desire for martyrdom. It is God's word (see Luke 21:12–18). We have to face this. And we can face it only on one condition, which I really want us to understand.

God calls to us,

"Comfort, comfort my people,
   says your God.
Speak tenderly to Jerusalem,
   and proclaim to her
that her hard service has been completed,
   that her sin has been paid for."

(Isaiah 40:1–2)

I know that it causes offence when Europeans speak to the Jewish people about their sin, in the light of our own history of guilt toward them. Nevertheless there is a way this can be done. It begins in our own personal lives.

Who is called to comfort?

Only those who can say, "This king is my king. This Father has become my Father" will be able to comfort. This is not an easy matter. In order to call this king my king I must reach the point where I can confess, "Lord, there is absolutely nothing good within me!"

In Romans 3:10–12 we read,

> " *'There is no one righteous, not even one;*
>   *there is no one who understands,*
>   *no one who seeks God.*
> *All have turned away,*
>   *they have together become worthless;*
> *there is no one who does good,*
>   *not even one.'* "

Today we would think this refers to war criminals, to arch terrorists, to deformed offspring of evil.

> " *'Their throats are open graves;*
>   *their tongues practice deceit.'*
> *'The poison of vipers is on their lips.*
>   *Their mouths are full of cursing and bitterness.'*
> *'Their feet are swift to shed blood;*
>   *ruin and misery mark their ways,*
> *and the way of peace they do not know.'*
>   *'There is no fear of God before their eyes.'* "

(Romans 3:13–18)

But it is more: it is an evaluation of the human heart itself.

It was often asked in view of the outrages committed in the Kosovo war, "How is it possible that people can cause others so much suffering, just slaughtering them?" I shocked my conversation partners by saying that I would also be capable of doing all these things. If I weren't living under God's grace and were left to myself, I would be capable of it. According to Genesis 8:21 my heart is evil from my youth. That is the truth.

A person who has not acknowledged this will never really comprehend that the cross is absolutely necessary for his salvation, his liberation and his healing. He will never comprehend what guilt really means and thus also never comprehend what forgiveness is, in other words, what took place on the cross. Then we will never find the Father, nor will we have a testimony for the Jewish people.

Waiting for the Prince of Peace

It is not a triumphant matter to be a disciple of this king, this Messiah of Israel. For what sort of king is he? It is said of him, *"He is humble, riding on the foal of a donkey."* In Matthew 22 Jesus says of himself, *"Come to me, learn from me, for I am gentle and humble in heart."*

Every person who comes to this Messiah must ask himself, "Am I ready to serve such a king? Am I willing to have my life changed by the rule of this king? Have I allowed this king to break all my instruments of battle?"

If this does not happen, the Messiah cannot become a testimony through us to the Jewish people. This people is still looking for a king, one who will break the instruments of battle and remove the war horses. This begins in the personal lives of all those who place themselves under his rule.

When I look into congregations and families, I often realize that we are all armed to the teeth! The goal is always to use these weapons to create our own righteousness, our own living space, our own confirmation. Each one has developed his own weapons in order to keep others at a distance, to make them submit and to take advantage of them, or to "manipulate them into" his own plans. Leaders do this with their team members and vice versa, parents with their children and vice versa, marriage partners with each other . . .

The Gospel has to do with our real lives, not with religion and dogmas. If a believer's life is not changed by the Gospel, he has avoided a genuine encounter with it.

When this king, this Messiah comes, he will change our lives and lead us into God's reality. Breaking the instruments of battle means that I permit the Messiah to disarm me in all my relationships. If I want to enter the Father's house, I must relinquish my weapons to the Messiah at the door. I cannot get into God's heart if I am armed.

Seeds of the kingdom of heaven

The problem is that with a few exceptions, the Jewish people has never experienced the Church as the one who is at God's heart. The Church is seen fighting for power and prestige, for positions, influence, and authority. In order to truly sow the seeds of the kingdom of heaven among the Jewish people, God must first make his kingdom a reality in our hearts and in our midst. Then he can make a path to his people through our hearts.

God longs to find people who are willing to do this work of the heart and say, "I will let myself be sent by the one who said of himself, '*As the Father sent me, so I send you*'" (John 20:21).

The Messiah always wants to reveal the Father's heart. He wants to send us just as he was sent, so that the Father can be recognized by the way we relate to one another. The Jewish people are longing for the reality of God's kingdom, not for religion.

The secular Jews I talk with reject everything which has to
do with religion. But when they see people relating to each
other, when they see sound families, they begin asking, "How
do you do it? Where does this atmosphere come from – this
order, this peace?"

They want to experience God's reality as described by the
apostle John,

> "*That which was from the beginning, which we have heard,
> which we have seen with our eyes, which we have looked at
> and our hands have touched – this we proclaim concerning the
> Word of life.*"
>
> (1 John 1:1)

Not what we have heard third or fourth hand, but what has
become a reality in our lives.

Tangible fatherhood

Can we say, "I have a Father, I'm at home with him, I am held
securely"? Is this a genuine reality for me or am I still looking
for my identity, for my place, for the answer to the question,
"Who am I really and what should I do?"

If we haven't come to the Father, are not at home with him,
do not live in a deep and trusting relationship with him, do not
know that we have everything in the Messiah – what do we
want to tell the Jewish people? Then we will be those who are
only concerned about our own needs, instead of messengers
who bring support, help and hope.

Some Christians convert to Judaism because they have not
understood that they have already received everything from
the Messiah. However, we will not gain Jewish people's
attention by becoming as Jewish as possible.

Only a person who has come to the Father, who can say that

Jesus is his Messiah and king, the person in whose life this can be seen and felt – only such a person is capable of touching the greatly wounded heart of the Jewish people.

"The Jews first"

The Gospel is first of all for the Jewish people, even if the Church has taught for centuries, "The Jewish people last" and today even says, "The Jews not at all!" But God's Word says "first", not "last"! Why?

The Gospel is Jewish! God has given it to this people and he is waiting for them to discover how close their greatest treasure is. He says, *"Comfort my people, tell them the good news."*

This is not a proselytizing crusade! It is not setting something foreign on the Jewish people or pulling it out of its calling, of capturing it and making it into Church members. One can do nothing more precious for the Jewish people than tell them about the Messiah. That is what God's Word says.

God is longing for the Jewish people to deeply experience that he is the Father of Israel. And no one but the Messiah can lead to the Father. There is no other way, not even for the Jewish people!

The Messiah says, "I have come to reveal the Father and lead you to him." Truth and grace became flesh in him.

If someone wishes to be sent as Jesus was sent from the Father, he must first learn to put up with mistrust, distance, and rejection. For this is how the Jewish people's wounded heart, distrustful from thousands of negative experiences, will initially react to every form of testimony. This wounded heart must perceive nearness and warmth, in spite of all that. It is a great challenge to truly embrace the Jewish people so that they may experience God's love and warmth.

God is waiting for those whose love for him moves them to tell his people about him; for there is nothing he desires more than that his people call him "Father" through the Messiah. We do this, yes because we know the Jewish people have a central place in salvation history, but first and foremost out of love for him.

The Jewish people need our testimony

In our relationship to Israel, we should not look only at its borders and at politics. We should concentrate on the condition of the society, on this people's battle and needs.

Since the enemy did not succeed in eradicating the Jewish people from without, he is now attempting to do so from within. The abortion rate is alarming. In some schools homosexuality has been officially recognized as a valid lifestyle; Israel's president was attacked and called to account because he very cautiously said something against the homosexual life style. In addition, there are tensions and sometimes hatred between various groups. There is a massive increase in violence and crime.

We must plead in prayer that Israel will not be destroyed from within, that the messianic body will become light to the world. We need to pray that families in this society will become a blessing through their life.

We must pray that through us, people will experience that God is really the Father, that they will receive hope for their relationships, for their circumstances, for their future. We can do this only if even after the first, second, and third slap in the face we do not sever the relationship, if we do not give up when insulted. We must continue seeking out the wounded heart behind the thick walls of defense.

This can cost our reputation, our possessions, our well-being, or even our life. God's comfort is not cheap. It cost Jesus his life. It will also cost us a great deal – not only here in the land, but also in our homeland if the Church and the tide of humanistic public opinion rise against us. There is a price to pay.

Am I willing to sow?

Do I really want fruit to grow? If I speak of a harvest, what am I willing to sow among this people through my own life? What have I invested so far outside of a visit to the country? Where have I sought God's heart – not my own concepts and desires for this people – with all my energy? Am I discouraged by those who think my efforts are hopeless?

Before we speak of a harvest in Israel we must allow the Holy Spirit to illuminate our own lives. There are many Christians who come here, who even participate in a messianic congregation, but who are a great burden instead of a help. Instead of bringing comfort from God's heart, they themselves are looking for comfort. They are like leeches – here, where there is so much need.

May the people who come here experience God's comfort in their own hearts, so that they can truly comfort others!

Chapter 8

Overcoming Evil

In May 2001, I visited the extermination camp Auschwitz-Birkenau in Poland with a group of Jewish congregational leaders. Within two years, 1.75 million Jews were murdered in this place of unimaginable horror. But Auschwitz is more than one of the darkest chapters in the history of mankind. What happened here sixty years ago still raises existential questions, which we as Christians can no longer afford to avoid or suppress.

When confronted with an unimaginable machinery of cruelty, humiliation, torture, death, and degradation at Auchwitz, one is inevitably confronted with questions. How is such a thing possible? How could man become a demon toward man? How can people go as far as to misuse children for medical experiments, exposing them to unspeakable pain and mental torture, only to destroy them afterwards? How is it possible that educated, cultured men, themselves family fathers, simultaneously embody evil?

In these rooms of horror I realized how difficult it is to allow one's heart to be touched by the reality of evil which is so obvious in Auschwitz. I began to understand that neo-Nazis, right-wing extremists, and anti-Semites are not the only

Holocaust deniers. There is also a form of Holocaust denial among Jews and Christians.

It is not that the literal facts of the Holocaust are denied, but that one refuses to deal with the pain and the reality of the unfathomable evil expressed here. We have to ask ourselves the reason for it.

When dealing with the question of how such a degree of evil was possible in the Nazi Holocaust, some say it was simply a German phenomenon. Others may imagine that such a thing could not take place in our current day. This is an understandable response, but one which must be answered with a clear No.

Shortly before my trip to Auschwitz I read an article in the French daily *Le Monde*, with excerpts from a newly released biography of a French general. He described with repulsive objectivity how during the French-Algerian war he tortured and killed hundreds of people. These acts were committed without emotion, neither compassion nor hatred. He regretted only that many died without divulging the desired information. He simply did his job, which consisted of torturing and killing.

We think of the genocides at the beginning of the twentieth century in which the Turks murdered 1.5 million Armenians. In the 1970s, more than a million people were murdered in Cambodia under Pol Pot. In the Soviet Gulag millions likewise lost their lives. This was followed in the 1990s by massacres in Rwanda and Burundi, Bosnia, Serbia, and Kosovo. In total over the twentieth century millions of people were humiliated, tortured, and in the end put to death.

Silence is also guilt

What we find concentrated in Auschwitz is a universal pattern which throughout history has repeatedly surfaced all over the world. It is very tempting to reduce this pattern to individual types of persons or certain peoples.

For example, one could object that peace-loving Switzerland had nothing to do with concentration and extermination camps. But it has been proven that the Swiss government and part of the population knew of the deportations and murder of Jews. They failed to oppose this, which amounts to condoning Nazi behavior.

The borders were closed to Jewish refugees and thousands were sent to their death. The grandparents of a close friend of mine were turned away at the Swiss-French border. They were immediately arrested by the Germans and perished in the gas chambers of Auschwitz.

We must clearly state that all those in Switzerland, in Europe, in Canada and the USA who knew of the Nazi crimes and nevertheless turned people back were no less a part of the horrors which took place. Their silence made them just as guilty as those who were the direct instruments of evil.

And here we have the same question: Why? How is this possible in a civilized society which could have learned a different lesson from history?

Western nations, including believers, should have become sensitized by the 2,000-year history of Jewish persecution. It cannot be said that they were taken by surprise by the way Jews were beginning to be treated in Germany. Anti-Semitic tendencies had become increasingly manifest, without being given due attention.

We must be cautious about saying that something like the Holocaust could never happen again. For it is exactly the Holocaust which testifies to the fact that man does not learn from history, even from Jewish history. Man does not learn from the knowledge of what has happened, not even from his own experience. He learns only when he consciously deals with the root and cause and becomes aware of his own susceptibility to evil.

We must learn to understand in depth how evil could and still can become so prevalent.

There is no such thing as the "good person"

During our visit to the extermination camp in Auschwitz, God reminded me again of the third chapter of Romans. I read what Paul wrote about Jews and heathen:

> " *'There is no one righteous, not even one;*
> *there is no one who understands,*
> *no one who seeks God.*
> *All have turned away,*
> *they have together become worthless;*
> *there is no one who does good,*
> *not even one.'*
> *'Their throats are open graves;*
> *their tongues practice deceit.'*
> *'The poison of vipers is on their lips.*
> *Their mouths are full of cursing and bitterness.'*
> *'Their feet are swift to shed blood;*
> *ruin and misery mark their ways,*
> *and the way of peace they do not know.'*
> *'There is no fear of God before their eyes.'* "
>
> (Romans 3:10–18)

This is exactly how we picture an SS officer, a person ruled by evil. But this description was not written for the Nazis. It applies without exception to every person. If we believed these words in the depths of our hearts they would jolt us with an overwhelming shock.

We are quickly tempted to reduce the reality of evil to

persons in whom it is obviously manifest, for example Hitler and his helpers, i.e. a few individuals who were totally penetrated by evil, who set Nazi Germany's death machinery in motion. To some extent we attempt to excuse the others, who blindly carried out these orders or who were silent.

But God's Word tells us that evil is in the heart of every person.

> *"Every inclination of* [man's] *heart is evil from childhood."*
> (Genesis 8:21)

Because evil hates God it wants to rule over fallen creation, destroy everything in it which reminds us of God and bears his image. The devil wants to transform man who was created in God's image into its own image. In other words, man makes himself the center and the standard of all things.

Pride and arrogance, nourished by deep inferiority feelings, become the source of contempt, violence, terror, merciless-ness, and cruelty. By determining death and destruction, man thinks he can control life. That is the nature of evil.

Auschwitz demonstrates in concentrated form the fact that evil seeks to destroy life. During World War II millions of people were murdered in the extermination camps by men without inner involvement and without feelings, except for the satisfaction of exercising power.

This exposes the true nature of evil: killing people without compassion and without hatred, with an uninvolved heart. It is almost impossible to imagine that concentration camp commanders were caring family fathers, tending their homes and gardens, enjoying beautiful music, interested in theater and art – and simultaneously destroying life in an absolutely evil and merciless way.

This demonstrates the extent to which evil can take over a person who is not living under God's control. Auschwitz is obvious proof that there is no such thing as a good person. The cultivated, educated person is not the good person, even if we often try to make this connection. Nor does Western civilization express the reality of goodness in man.

A disastrous error

We must be sober and aware of the power of evil and its grip on the human heart, so that we can warn those around us. Above all we must ask how we can overcome evil. Because evil is a reality in each one of us, the darkness, the cruelty, the absolute malevolence of a Holocaust can repeat itself at any time.

It is a disastrous error to believe that the Holocaust is a thing of the past for our nations, whether directly or indirectly involved. We may not think that it may finally be put behind us because it obviously cannot be repeated. Evil is a reality of the human heart and will keep taking over the person who does not actively resist it.

Evil comes violently

Because evil comes in the form of violence it can enter persons who fear for their own lives. Its demand is clear: If we do not submit and comply we will lose our lives. Hundreds of thousands in Nazi Germany and surrounding countries were silent or complied, even though they sensed that it was not right.

Satan knows that a person will do anything to save his own life and the lives of his loved ones. If the pressure is great enough and a person fears for his life, he will submit.

Sometimes even anxiety over one's material existence is sufficient to make a person submit to the dictate of violence. How else can it be explained that in Germany so many educated people, who were surely not without a conscience, could go as far as to torture, murder, and destroy others?

Revelation 12:11 shows how the enemy can be overcome, namely by those *"who do not love their lives so much as to shrink from death."* As long as we are fighting for our lives we are an easy prey for evil, no matter what our spiritual knowledge, experiences, or gifts.

Fear for one's life begins with little things. We're afraid to lose face. We're afraid of ridicule. We're afraid of being ostracized because we're considered narrow-minded, intolerant, fundamentalist, religious crazies, beyond common sense. We fear for our success. We are afraid we could lose something meaningful, for example our own undamaged reputation.

If we shrink back from enmity now and dare not commit ourselves to the truth, to take a stand for Jesus and the Jewish people, for God's Word and plan, we will submit all the more when matters get serious.

Therefore we must ask ourselves if there is something in our lives which we cannot relinquish. We know from Matthew 24 that darkness is not behind us, but ahead of us. Jesus said that lawlessness and evil would take over and that *"love would grow cold in many."*

These persons can be overcome by the devil because they do not cling to the cross but to their own lives and the things which bind them to this world. What haven't people done to save their own lives?

The open gate of inferiority feelings

A second open gate for evil is inferiority. A person who is not sure of his own worth and identity will be threatened by whatever is strange and different, but also by weakness and misery, which reminds him of his own weakness. These inferiority feelings lead to pride and arrogance. A person makes himself the standard.

Because of inferiority feelings, people make lists of rank

which define each individual's worth. It is a small step from classifying people to degrading them.

Every person has a capability for such behavior. Thus the devil can lead people through their inferiority feelings into such arrogance that they think in terms of ruling and slave races. They decide which life should be developed and which life eliminated because it is ill, weak, or unusual.

Along with the Jews, many Gypsies as well as many invalids and physically and mentally handicapped people were murdered. Hatred was shown for the poor and miserable, in effect deriding God, their Creator. As Proverbs 17:5 tells us, *"He who mocks the poor shows contempt for their Maker."*

The Church's need of salvation

The Holocaust revealed not only the reality of evil but also the necessity of man's salvation. Moreover, the Holocaust reveals how much the Church with all its denominations and theologies needs salvation.

Had the Church taken a clear stand then, the enemy could not have so easily reduced it to silence, even using it as one of his instruments of destruction. When the trains packed with Jews rolled through Auschwitz on their way to the concentration camps, the cries of these people could be heard in the town. It is known that some priests told their congregations to sing louder so that these cries could no longer be heard.

Not only in Germany, but also in Switzerland and other near-by countries the majority of churches knew of the Nazi crimes, but most of them were silent. When we are silent regarding evil, it creeps into our hearts and takes over.

The Church and all of us who know Jesus as Lord must again be aware of the necessity of experiencing and living salvation. We must return to the cross. Only at the cross is evil destroyed. Only at the cross does evil lose access to people.

This means that we must realize how much we ourselves need salvation. We must accept our own capacity for sin and pray from our hearts, "Lord, deliver us from evil!"

The devil wants to separate us from God, and thus from our brother as well. Evil is everything which directs our acts and thoughts to ourselves, making a priority of our own needs and goals. It is everything which makes us indifferent to our brother.

Evil always causes us to take sin lightly. Sin is not primarily moral misbehavior, but lack of love and willingness to forgive in our daily lives. It is the readiness with which we think negatively and disparagingly of one another, suspecting others of bad intentions.

Sin is our refusal to demonstrate to our brothers and sisters, whoever they are, that God is unconditionally for them. It is sin when we hurt a neighbor and then leave him with the wound, or when we grow bitter toward others and do not attempt to settle the matter.

It is sin when we set our own judgment of our environment and the world's attitudes above God's Word and command. When we take sin lightly and do not resist evil in small matters, we will have little with which to counter it when things become serious.

The "ten righteous"

I was deeply moved to see that in Auschwitz and other concentration camps some people overcame evil through their lives and deaths because they resisted it from the beginning. They did not love their lives, but even in such places gave themselves for others.

These were persons who in spite of violence, torture, and humiliation gave no room to hatred or bitterness. Thanks to their relationship with Jesus their dignity and value could not be destroyed. In this hell, these few persons became signs of hope, although perhaps not many were aware of it.

A German pastor once asked why God did not give Germany over to destruction after such a monstrous crime. I am convinced that it is because God found his "ten righteous" in Germany – men and women who voluntarily gave their lives for others.

They could have kept silent and thus saved their lives, like all the others. But resistance to the power of evil is possible, as these brothers and sisters demonstrated, even if they went through atrocities and forfeited their lives. They thus testified that the devil cannot destroy what Jesus creates in a person's life. This gives hope.

We cannot assume that we will never encounter similar situations in the future. But we can pray from our hearts that even now we will not allow ourselves to be overcome by any evil in our daily lives. We can pray that we will counter evil with the same testimony as these "ten righteous." This is the testimony that God cares for our lives, our dignity, our security, and that no one can rob what Jesus created in our lives.

Scapegoat Israel

Just as the cross must be the center of the Church, Israel can likewise be saved from evil only through the cross. Even though the Jews are God's chosen people, these persons are just as liable to evil as any others.

We have to see clearly that the enemy tries with all his means to stamp his image on this people. In the controversy with the Palestinians, bringing the experience of terror and violence, Israel is in danger of being drawn into the same spiral of hatred, bitterness, and violence.

All the more must we Christians be cautious not to support the world's sense of justice. As the world plays the advocate of the weak and the victims, it is calling Israel the aggressor or "Goliath," and pleading for peace.

The Near East conflict is reduced to the image of a heavily armed army with tanks against stone-throwing children and believers are told that it is a Christian command to take the side of the oppressed. The Jewish state is the scapegoat of the conflict, the side which is seen as hindering justice and peace.

The negative, one-sided stand of the EU, the UNO, and many individual countries toward Israel should make us stop and think. Wasn't it just like this before World War II, when the Jews were also scapegoated? They were painted as the ones who took away jobs, ruled finances, and planned some sort of power ploys. But now it is not the Jews as such who have the scapegoat role, but the state of Israel.

When we think of how the EU, the UNO and the nations have refrained from exercising justice in the face of atrocities and human rights violations in Islamic countries – as well as Africa, Russia, China, and Asia – and what standard is laid on Israel (of course in the name of justice), we could become ill from the stench of hypocrisy.

The demand for justice is legitimate and necessary. But when that demand is made only of Israel, and seldom or never of the political and religious Palestinian leadership, there is something suspect. When the daily calls via TV, radio, and newspapers for hatred, violence, and murder of the Jewish people are excused and justified, we sense that this attitude is less a matter of justice than of the old spirit which accuses the Jews, this time through Israel.

The voice of the Church

It is depressing how often the Church's voice can be heard at the forefront of this one-sided accusation of Israel. The state of Israel is not perfect. There are mistakes, omissions, injustice, pride, arrogance. But which country, which individual, after looking into their own hearts, can throw the first stone?

Israel can be and should be criticized, but only by those who apply the same standard of justice to themselves and to other peoples. The state of Israel, and with it the Jewish people, must not again become the scapegoat for the nations' impotence and failure.

Today it takes courage for a Christian to firmly resist the superficial and thoughtless slogans about justice which fan enmity toward Israel. Many will cry that we are intolerant, narrow-minded, and unjust. We must find the courage to stand up for the truth through the word of our testimony, as we read in Revelation 12:11.

We don't wish to make our own opinion, our own interpretation of history and politics the standard, but rather the authority of God's Word. We know that it is a God of life who sovereignly chose the Jewish people and promised them the land. He will save Israel and make them a blessing for all peoples.

If the Church does not realize which door evil seeks to enter, it will end where it was during World War II. This Church which with few exceptions did not resist evil, terribly damaged its testimony to the Jewish people.

In the face of developments in Germany, Switzerland, and the rest of Europe, there is no reason to assume that the Holocaust will not be repeated in coming days. On the contrary, I believe that quite soon the Church will receive a second chance in its relationship to the Jewish people.

When that happens, the Church will be able to demonstrate whether it still wants to be part of the silent majority, full of good humanistic arguments against Israel and the Jewish people. Or alternatively, Christians can show whether they choose to be among those who *"overcame [the devil] by the blood of the Lamb and by the word of their testimony, they did not love their lives so much as to shrink from death"* (Revelation 12:11).

Hope and the future

Back to Auschwitz. As we were standing in those gas chambers and crematoria, praying and singing, it moved me to realize again that the devil does not attain his goals. Sixty years later we stand in this place and declare that there is a future for the Jewish people and for every person who comes to Jesus.

We want to proclaim this future and this hope in our lives to the Jewish people and out into the world: There is a future and there is a hope – but only on the basis of the cross.

Chapter 9

The Book of Ruth: The Church's Responsibility to the Jewish People

Today the book of Ruth can help us more deeply understand the relationship between the Church and the Jewish people. It illustrates how the Church can help Israel find the way back to her God and how believers in the nations can thus grow into a deeper relationship with their Messiah. The book of Ruth shows us clearly how to fulfill God's command, *"Comfort, comfort my people"* (Isaiah 40:1).

Naomi, who in her suffering had turned away from God, represents better than any other figure the Jewish people of today. In her bitterness, her distance from God and, finally, her return to him, she is a parable of Israel. Ruth, on the other hand, is a picture of the Church which through its confession and its love for the God of Israel, the God of Naomi, is grafted into the covenant God made with his people.

At first glance the story seems simple. During the time of the judges, a man named Elimelech lived in Bethlehem with his wife Naomi and his two sons, Mahlon and Kilion. When a famine came upon the land of Israel he decided to leave Bethlehem and move to Moab, a foreign country, to ensure his family's survival.

The name Elimelech means "my God reigns" and his wife's name Naomi means "pleasant." So Elimelech was a man who lived under God's reign and under this reign he was given pleasure. It is no coincidence that Elimelech lived in Bethlehem, which means "the house of bread," because where God reigns he promises his life and his provision.

The names of the sons of Naomi and Elimelech are also meaningful, however. Mahlon means "illness, weakness" and Kilion means "consumption, destruction."

Elimelech, who lived under God's reign in Bethlehem, the house of bread, was confronted with famine and illness. Something broke into his life which drove him and his wife Naomi out of the house of bread and into a foreign place. There Naomi lost everything: God's reign ended, her husband and sons died and she was left poorer than in Bethlehem. She was alone.

At this point we can ask ourselves, "Who gives us life?" From whom do we expect help when we are afflicted by illness and problems, when our emotions try to tell us that there will be no more bread, that God is no longer caring for us? We have all experienced situations where we ask ourselves, "Where is God?"

Leaving God's dominion

Naomi and Elimelech's departure from Bethlehem illustrates the history of the Jews. Israel was called to live under God's reign and in his provision. God promised the Jewish people that their bread would never run out, and that he would protect them from illness and miscarriage if they remained in him (as we see in Leviticus and Deuteronomy).

During the course of Israel's history, illness, drought and failure were always rooted in the fact that the people did not truly submit to God's reign. Whenever they had such problems, the people of Israel had let themselves be driven out of the place of God's dominion. They had departed from their "house of bread" – just as Elimelech and Naomi had departed from Bethlehem many years earlier.

Because Elimelech and Naomi no longer believed in the provision of their heavenly father, they sought life in a foreign place where God did not reign. Israelites understood that God did not reign in Moabite people, but another god reigned over them. Even if Elimelech and Naomi were not aware of it, they thus placed themselves under the authority of a foreign god, expecting help and life from him.

In the first book of Samuel we read of Israel's desire to be like all the other nations. It was willing to leave its own inheritance in order to draw from the wells of life among others, thus placing herself under the reign of other gods. *"Now appoint a king to lead us, such as all the other nations have"* (1 Samuel 8:5).

This desire has characterized Israel to the present day. The Jewish people are still drawing life and orientation from all sorts of wells, always with disastrous consequences. In the end they are like Naomi, bitter, poor and empty, having lost infinitely more than they gained.

We can also see Israel's behavior in our own lives. How often have we placed ourselves under the reign of other authorities and powers in order to find some sort of satisfaction and life? The results are clear: If we allow our needs and problems to drive us away from God's reign, if we leave his provision and seek help elsewhere, we will lose everything. For in the foreign place, under the reign of another god, there is only destruction and death.

Back to Bethlehem, the place of the inheritance

After the death of her husband and sons, Naomi decided to return to the house of her fathers in Bethlehem. She who had departed in hope had to return as an absolute failure, poor and naked, but she returned. On the one hand this was a miracle, but on the other hand it has to be so, because Israel must always return to the place of inheritance.

It is the calling and destiny of the Jewish people to come home. Wherever Israel wanders, whatever judgments it endures, it will have to return to the place of inheritance. Whether they want it or not, there is no other place for the Jews – and God is waiting there for his people.

Naomi returned home but she despaired of coming back to life in her homeland. She held God responsible for everything she had experienced: *"The LORD's hand has gone out against me!"* (Ruth 1:13). When greeted in Bethlehem, she said, *"Don't call me Naomi, call me Mara, because the Almighty has made my life very bitter"* (Ruth 1:20).

Her accusation is bitter, exactly like the Jewish people today. Their questions are full of deep bitterness over the loss of their land, their possessions, their sons and daughters, their inheritance. Where was God in the Holocaust? Where was God in the pogroms? Where was God during the centuries, during the millennia?

This bitterness has made the Jewish people feel very hopeless about God. Even the religious do not expect God to move concretely in their lives. Faith has been reduced to external rituals and forms and often lacks any sense of a personal relationship with God.

This is evident in Israel's present difficult situation. Hardly any religious leader, let alone a political one, has stood up and called on the people to pray, turn to the God of Israel and look to him for help. The fact that God is hardly mentioned in the current situation shows that the Jewish people, apart from a small minority, are like Naomi. They no longer expect anything from God, but are deeply bitter.

Ruth: a picture of the Church

"Don't urge me to leave you or to turn back from you. Where you go I will go, and where you stay I will stay. Your people will be my people and your God my God."

(Ruth 1:16)

Because Naomi's daughter-in-law Ruth came from heathen Moab, she is a picture of the gentile Church, the believers from the nations. Somehow in spite of Naomi's struggle and suffering, Ruth is able to recognize the God of Israel. Jesus would have recognized in her a woman of truth.

"Everyone on the side of truth listens to me."

(John 18:37)

It is ultimately a mystery why anyone is of the truth. In spite of Naomi's disappointment and bitterness, Ruth discovered that Naomi's God was not like her own pagan god, *Kamosh*, nor any other gods known to her.

Rahab of Jericho

Ruth was given the same revelation as Rahab of Jericho. Rahab also lived under the reign of other gods but came to the conclusion that the God of Israel must be the only living God. This led her to take the side of this God and his people.

Convinced that the God of Israel would be victorious and would reach his goal with his covenant people, she decided to hide the spies and to put her life in their hands. When Jericho was conquered by the Israelites she was saved because she had tied the red cord in her window as a sign.

It was not by chance that the color red was chosen. It was the sign that there was only one way Rahab could be saved. It stood for blood and sacrifice, for the blood which saved Israel from the death of the firstborn in Egypt. It also stands for the blood of Jesus, through which all peoples can participate in the promises to Israel and its inheritance.

Like Ruth, Rahab the prostitute was a woman of truth. Because she listened to God's voice and was obedient, she became an ancestor of David and belongs to the direct line of the Messiah.

Ruth was also saved because she was obedient to God, but there is even more to be seen in her life. By bringing Naomi's dead faith back to life, she made it possible for Naomi to gain her inheritance. Figuratively speaking, Ruth helped the Jewish people gain access to their own inheritance. She became a key figure for the Jews.

Rare characteristics

In Ruth we notice certain rare characteristics. Her faithfulness to her mother-in-law is more than a matter of a kind heart and love for Naomi. Ruth's faithfulness cost her everything: her own inheritance, her own people, in fact everything which had formerly been part of her life.

She anticipated what the prophet Jeremiah later said,

> "O LORD, my strength and my fortress,
>   my refuge in time of distress,
> to you the nations will come
>   from the ends of the earth and say,
> 'Our fathers possessed nothing but false gods,
>   worthless idols that did them no good.'"

(Jeremiah 16:19)

Ruth realized that the inheritance of her fathers had no substance because it lacked any personal relationship to the living God. Therefore she left her inheritance and with it everything which had previously given her security and protection. She turned to the God of Israel and his covenant people.

She came to this people as a foreigner and could only count on God's mercy. Without a husband, merely as the companion of her mother-in-law, she had no guarantee that she would be accepted. But she was confident that Naomi's God was also her God and that he would restore to her everything she had left behind.

Ruth was not only faithful, but also humble and modest. For her mother-in-law's sake she was willing to take her place as a recipient among the Israelites. She gleaned the fields as a beggar, widow or orphan would have done. She demanded no rights, made no claims and did not strive for recognition, appreciation or gratitude.

She listened to her mother-in-law, submitted to her, and renounced her own ideas. It is written that she gleaned all day until sunset. She invested her whole life in the fields by working more than the other servants. Her attitude is an example to all Christians who wish to serve the Jewish people.

Ruth and the Savior

Boaz, the owner of the field where Ruth worked, is a picture of the Messiah. The servants and the local people didn't notice Ruth, but Boaz noticed her and took an interest in her. He asked about her, gave her food and promised to protect her. As a result of this encounter and provision, she returned to Naomi in the evening richly blessed.

None of this escaped Naomi's notice. She saw the blessing and realized that Ruth had had a special, unexpected encounter, so she asked, *"Where did you glean today? Where did you work? Blessed be the man who took notice of you!"* (Ruth 2:19).

Ruth – and as we now see, the Church, the congregation, the

believers from the nations – had met the owner of the field, the owner of the inheritance, and she had received riches. That was obvious to Naomi and brought her to say for the first time, *"The Lord bless him, who has not stopped showing his kindness"* (Ruth 2:20).

Suddenly Naomi began to recognize God. She understood that the God of Israel had not deserted her. She remembered that Boaz was her relative. He was not only a kinsman but also the "kinsman-redeemer," the savior who held the answer to her needs.

This same process of recognition is taking place among the Jewish people today. They wake up as the believing Church firmly stands with them, saying, *"Your God is my God, your people is my people."*

As the body of Christ makes this confession, it can overcome every form of rejection, bitterness and misunderstanding that it encounters. The riches God gave to the Church are carried into its relationship with the Jewish people through such faithfulness and obedience. This catches the Jews' attention and they realize, "The One who enriched the Church has something to do with us, after all! We know him!" They discover that Jesus was a Jew!

As a result of Christians' positive attitude toward the Jewish population, many rabbis in the USA recently decided that they must take a new look at Jesus, for the Christians believe in the same God they do.

The Jewish people who return to their inheritance need a Ruth to draw their attention to this Redeemer. They need a Ruth who has decided to stand by this people who cannot see God – an embittered people without a future.

Closer to the Messiah

Naomi began to hope again and told Ruth how to build a closer relationship with the kinsman-redeemer. Again Ruth humbly heeded Naomi's advice. But for the body of Christ it is difficult to listen like this.

For the past two thousand years, there has been little interest by the Church in the Jewish people and the Jewish roots of the Gospel. Consciously or not, many Christians assume that today the Jews have no great meaning and therefore little to say. This attitude of the Church is proud and arrogant, resulting even in a claim to the inheritance that rightly belongs to Israel – all because of a tragic misunderstanding.

God commissions the believers in the nations to comfort his covenant people (Isaiah 40:1) and show them the way to their God by applying the promise in Jeremiah 31:33. This is the heart covenant that Jesus made on the cross.

God wants his covenant people to perceive in the lives of Christians the face of the Father whom Jesus revealed. We are often unwilling to display this because we don't feel accountable to the Jewish people. In this way we obstruct our own path on which we could grow closer to Jesus.

Ruth took Naomi's advice to sit at Boaz's feet and wait until he woke up. She took the place of a servant and slave who slept at his master's feet. Ruth expressed her total dependence on Boaz. She demanded nothing, but behaved like the servants in Luke 17:10, *"When you have done everything you were told to do, say, 'We are unworthy servants; we have done only our duty.'"*

The Church should have the same attitude toward the Messiah that Ruth had towards Boaz. She was not to waken him but to wait until he awoke and turned to her. When Boaz awoke, Ruth said, *"Spread the corner of your garment over me"* (Ruth 3:9), which meant that she wanted him to marry her.

This request expressed, more than anything else, devotion and submission to the redeemer's authority. Ruth was not primarily interested in finding a husband. She accepted Naomi's advice that this man was the solution to her need and she humbled herself for Naomi's sake.

Ruth's marriage to Boaz would bring Naomi a future and a hope. Naomi would have descendants and a claim to the inheritance. Ruth's submission to the redeemer, her obedience and the dedication of her own life are linked with Naomi's inheritance.

The key to the inheritance

Ruth became the grandmother of David, from whose family the Messiah descended. David was a symbol of God's reign, which is the inheritance of the Jewish people.

God's reign was first established among the Jews and from them it was released over the whole creation. But this inheritance can be released only through the obedience, humility and service of the Church, the believers in the nations. The Church itself can live only in the inheritance that God has given to the Jews. As soon as the Church moves away from this inheritance, under the impression that she no longer needs it, she reverts to paganism, as church history clearly shows.

On the other hand, because of their history the Jewish people are incapable of releasing their inheritance. God in his wisdom ordained that the Church and the Jewish people would need each other.

In the letter to the Romans, Paul says that the salvation of the heathen is intended to make Israel jealous, i.e. to open the eyes of the Jews. When Israel becomes jealous, she recognizes that the heathen became rich through her inheritance, her God and the promises that were first given to her.

The Church is a key in God's hands, with which he wants to give the Jewish people access to their inheritance. In our days God is urgently calling believers from all the churches to take a stand for the Jewish people and become a key like Ruth.

During the past two thousand years God gave wisdom and riches to his Church. But that is not everything! When the

Jewish people receives its inheritance, this salvation will affect all of creation. Everything else was only a prelude.

When the Jewish people recognize their Messiah Jesus, it will be only the beginning.

> *"For if their rejection is the reconciliation of the world, what will their acceptance be but life from the dead?"*
>
> (Romans 11:15)

Chapter 10

At the Crossroads

Political, economic and ideological developments increasingly demand a clear stand and evaluation from the Jewish people, from Israel as a state, and also from the Church of Christ.

Globalization makes the present world like the Tower of Babel. The Tower represented an increasingly cohesive and mutually dependent organization which was at the same time very vulnerable and whose survival was in danger.

The fusion of resources and power (e.g. worldwide economic agreements, military pacts, the standardization and co-ordination of educational programs) and the integration of peoples in a world community are intended to preserve, strengthen and optimize mankind's quality of life. Better control is supposed to reduce differences, with their resulting conflicts and tensions, and to harmonize our lives together in a transparent world community. Or so we are led to believe.

Israel is confronted with the oldest decision

Again Israel is confronted with the oldest of decisions, which has faced it ever since it was called to be God's people: Will it live as a people separated from the nations, a people fulfilling God's plans to be his witness, herald and priest? Will it hold fast to its calling and to the Promised Land – including all the tension-filled places such as Jerusalem, Hebron, Golan and Gaza?

If so, then Israel must accept the fact that in the eyes of the world community it is a stumbling block, a foreign body, a disastrous source of conflict. It always has been and always will be seen in this way. Therefore, as the nations see it, it must be eliminated for the sake of world peace.

The world offers Israel the guarantee of a secure, peaceful future if it integrates with the world community. It must renounce or at the least make more relative its very specific calling and claim to the land in order to harmonize with other nations.

Israel must decide: Either it submits to the reasoning and judgment of the world community, in order to receive a political peace, or it decides to obey God and his Word. It must agree to submit to the reign of our world powers or to God's reign.

Pressure on Israel is increasing

There is now unbelievable pressure on Israel and on the Jewish people. This pressure will increase if America one day ceases to be a protective world power (which could happen soon).

Israel is a stumbling block for the nations because it is a political incarnation of God's sovereignty; it is a warning and at the same time God's declaration of war against the rulers of this world which rebel against the rule of Israel's God and its Messiah (see Psalm 2).

God has separated Israel as an instrument to correct authority and power in his creation and to set them in the proper relations. He is the source of life and only in his light do the peoples see light (Psalm 36:10). Therefore, according to the second chapter of Isaiah, the nations will come to Zion for correction. What God has decided, he will carry out, in spite of all resistance (Isaiah 46:10).

Israel cannot avoid its calling

Israel cannot avoid its calling, for Israel did not choose God, God chose Israel. He is the one who acts, he is sovereign. Resisting him has only brought Israel unbelievable suffering and judgment up to the present day.

If Israel should ally itself with the world by making the world community's verdict its own standard, which would amount to rejecting its separate calling, it will continue to be painfully winnowed. This will happen until finally the holy, humble remnant of Israel appears, which will seek refuge in the name of its God (Zephaniah 3:12).

Israel must wholly accept its calling and, because it is a target of attack, take refuge in the hand of its God. Only then will it find peace and become a channel of blessing to the nations.

The Church of Jesus is, like Israel and with Israel, separated from the world.

> "If the world hates you, keep in mind that it hated me first. If you belonged to the world, it would love you as its own. As it is, you do not belong to the world, but I have chosen you out of the world. That is why the world hates you."
> (John 15:18–19).

In the same way, the Church did not choose the God of Israel. Nevertheless in his Messiah Jesus, God chose the Church so that she would go and bring fruit which honors the Father (John 15:16). The goal is that she would seek and establish the Father's honor in this world.

We read in Philippians 2:9–11,

> *"Therefore God exalted him to the highest place*
>   *and gave him the name that is above every name,*
> *that at the name of Jesus every knee should bow,*
>   *in heaven and on earth and under the earth,*
> *and every tongue confess that Jesus Christ is Lord,*
>   *to the glory of God the Father."*

The Church of Jesus must decide

We too, the Church of Jesus, must make a decision regarding our stand toward Israel and toward the world. This decision has the greatest import and effect. It is not only for our own life and identity as Jesus' Church, but ultimately for the relevance of our testimony in the world.

What testimony do we give the world? The testimony of the apostles John and Peter was that *"There is no other name under heaven given to men by which we must be saved"* (Acts 4:12). Do we confess with Paul that we know no other than the crucified Christ as the source of salvation, as the truth, as the answer to the need of the world? If so, then we will very quickly find ourselves on a collision course with the goals of the world community.

The harmonizing process set in motion to eliminate every form of peace-endangering conflicts will neither bear nor tolerate Jesus' claim, *"I am the way, the truth and the life. No one comes to the Father except through me"* (John 14:6).

Since many of the world's conflicts and wars are considered to have their origin in religion, every tension and difference between religions is closely observed. There is a willingness to grant a recognized, respected and equal place not only to Judaism, Christianity and Islam, but also to every form of religion. But this is only as long as they limit their absolute claim and authority to their own religious community and leave the rest of the world alone.

There is a place on the world stage for every religion which acknowledges that it serves mankind as just one truth among many truths. The world is willing to see religion just as a resource which can satisfy human intellectual, emotional, social and spiritual needs. This may fit religions that see themselves merely as cultural, traditional and ethnic identities that offer people an internal and an external framework for life.

But this is not acceptable for the Gospel. Across all cultures, traditions and ethnic groups the Gospel of Jesus Christ confronts individuals with their guilt before God. It confronts them with the fact that unless they bow before the atoning death of God's Son, there is no salvation, no rescue and no peace.

When the Gospel proclaims that Jesus is the truth, the way and the life, it testifies that all other "paths of salvation" are not truth, but false paths leading to death. What a stumbling block!

The Gospel is God's ultimate, absolute claim to the life of men; it stands like a boulder in the path of every effort to harmonize and equalize religion. Everyone who identifies with this message becomes a stumbling block and thus an enemy of the desired harmony and peace.

The world community, especially in the West, has made the fulfillment of man's needs and desires its goal. Biblical norms which previously regulated society according to God's commands are being increasingly discarded in order to make room for individual self-realization.

We as the Church of Jesus will very quickly be seen as enemies of man's freedom, self-realization and well-being if we reject the advance of relative values.

The fact is that if we insist that marriage and family are the cornerstone of society, as opposed to promiscuity and same-sex relationships, we will end up as outsiders. If we take a stand against abortion and stem cell research, challenging the human egoism that sacrifices others' lives, we will be ostracized. If we declare that euthanasia and publicly-sanctioned suicide cause guilt before God, we become out of step with our world's values.

Our calling: God's audible voice for the world

But only if we do these things will we retain our profile and remain God's audible voice for the world. One day this world will urgently cry for alternatives, help and refuge when – as Jesus says – love will grow cold in many because of increasing lawlessness.

Preserving God's love and keeping it accessible for the world, by not allowing the stumbling block of the cross to be moderated, has its price. Unlike Islam and other religions, we can never take up the sword for the Gospel. But if necessary, we like millions before us will give up our life under the sword so that the voice of God will not die away. Are we ready? May God give us grace!

The second decision we must make as the Church of Jesus has to do with Israel. God has begun to bring about the realization of his plans and promises for his people. After two thousand years of the Diaspora there is an Israeli state again. This is in spite of the resistance of the nations – and often of the Jewish people itself. It is in spite of the Church's resistance and lack of faith. The last chapter of God's history with mankind has been opened.

God's sovereignty is incarnated in and through his people Israel, arousing the resistance of the nations. His reign in the people and land reveals the heart attitude of the peoples toward God's rule. They react with rebellion, rejection and refusal. God's plans are proudly rejected, without understanding that his ways are always just and true.

The time of confrontation between God's sovereignty and the rulers of this world has come. Jerusalem, the city of the great king, becomes the cup of reeling and the basin of fire for the nations. There will be an increase of rebellion, hatred and enmity toward God and his Messiah, against his plans for the nations and for his people Israel.

This will all culminate in the fulfillment of Zechariah's prophecy (Zechariah 12:2–3), when the nations will gather in battle against the Messiah, against his city and against his people.

Will we as the Church of Jesus stand by Israel?

Where will the Church of Jesus then be? Will we obediently stand together with God and his plans for his people Israel? Will we stand by the Jewish people, thus making ourselves a target of hatred and enmity?

Just as God accepted us while we were still his enemies (Romans 11), drawing us to himself in love, so should the Church of Jesus wholeheartedly stand with the Jewish people and Israel. This is despite the fact that Israel has not yet broken through to its calling, God's glory is hardly visible and the people still grope in darkness in many aspects of their relationship to God.

We as the Church of Jesus will not stand by Israel because of human sympathy but because their God is our God, because their fathers have become our fathers and because Israel as God's people has become our people (Ephesians 2). It is unimportant how the world, the Church or even rabbinical Judaism sees this.

Through the Messiah Jesus, Israel has become our family. We stand by the Jewish people out of love and obedience toward Israel's God and toward Jesus, the King of the Jews. Whatever concerns Israel and the Jewish people must concern us as well.

Whenever the Church of Jesus allies herself with the world against God's plans for his people she betrays her Lord and his honor. For he himself says that the restoration of his people in the Promised Land serves the restoration of his honor (Ezekiel 36:22–23). The price the Church of Jesus will pay for standing by her Lord and his people Israel is irrelevant compared with the judgment she will experience if – united with the world – she betrays God.

God will not be prevented from fulfilling his plans. But woe to those who resist God's holy will, because they will face the holy anger which will fall upon all pride and arrogance. It will consume them.

The Church of Jesus belongs in the place where God's honor and that of his Messiah Jesus are at stake. Wherever his honor is established, the peoples will experience salvation, peace and rescue.

Do the Jews Need Jesus?

Ruben Berger

In conclusion we will return to a very basic question: Did Israel's meaning and calling come to an end when the Messiah came and the New Testament Church was established?

Do the Jewish people themselves really need the Gospel in order to find salvation? Or do they have direct access to the Father because they are the covenant people?

Many Christians do not agree about this and ask themselves whether evangelization among Jews is necessary and to what extent non-Jews even have the right to convey the Gospel to the Jewish people.

My friend Ruben Berger, a Messianic Jew, gives us an answer to this question.

Ruben grew up in an Orthodox Jewish family which experienced the atrocity of the Holocaust. In his search for the God of Israel, he realized that Jesus is really the Messiah in whom the promise for the Jewish people and for the whole world has begun to be fulfilled. This was in spite of the distorted picture of the Messiah Jesus which is normally conveyed to Jews.

Ruben and his brother Benjamin lead a congregation in Jerusalem.   *Marcel Rebiai*

Jesus – a Jew

Jesus, the Son of God and Savior of the world, was born into a Jewish family, raised according to Jewish tradition and lived according to the law in Scripture.

Jesus' message, preached to an almost exclusively Jewish audience, was clear: The law of Moses was inadequate to redeem mankind, he was the long-awaited Messiah and belief in him was necessary for a relationship with God. In addition, the apostles later explained that true forgiveness, salvation and inner transformation were possible only through a relationship with the Son of God.

Nevertheless, many Christians ask if the Jewish people need redemption through Jesus, just like everyone else. They wonder, in light of the tragic Holocaust and the poor testimony of the Church throughout the centuries, whether God really requires that the Jewish people believe in Jesus in order to receive salvation. The New Testament clearly answers these questions affirmatively.

Jesus – the redeemer of Israel

When Simeon, a righteous Jew who was *"waiting for the consolation of Israel,"* saw Jesus, he proclaimed,

> *"For my eyes have seen your salvation . . .*
> *a light for revelation to the Gentiles*
> *and for glory to your people Israel."*

(Luke 2:30, 32)

Paul said simply,

> *"I am not ashamed of the gospel, because it is the power of God*
> *for the salvation of everyone who believes: first for the Jew, then*
> *for the Gentile."*
>
> (Romans 1:16)

The writer to the Hebrews echoed this:

> *"For this reason Christ is the mediator of a new covenant, that*
> *those who are called may receive the promised eternal inherit-*
> *ance – now that he has died as a ransom to set them free from*
> *the sins committed under the first covenant."*
>
> (Hebrews 9:15)

The promise of a new covenant with God was originally
made to the house of Judah and the house of Israel.

> *" 'The time is coming,' declares the* LORD,
> *'when I will make a new covenant*
> *with the house of Israel*
> *and with the house of Judah.' "*
>
> (Jeremiah 31:31)

Only because Jesus is the redeemer of Israel can he be the
redeemer of all mankind and the world, as well. The Jewish
apostles understood this divine sequence when the Lord later
sent them to the Gentiles with the Gospel (Acts 13:46–49). The
blinding of the Jewish people and the hardening of their hearts
made it possible for salvation to be brought to all mankind.

God doesn't change his plans

Nevertheless, many Christians from the nations do not grasp
these central New Testament truths because their understanding

is not sufficiently rooted in God's Word. They are blind to the revelation of God's unique plan, which is his eternal relationship with Israel. This began with the covenants with Abraham and Moses and continues as the new covenant.

The writer of Hebrews confirms this continuation of God's plans,

> *"In the past God spoke to our forefathers through the prophets at many times and in various ways, but in these last days he has spoken to us by his Son, whom he has appointed heir of all things."*

> (Hebrews 1:1–2)

The guilt of the Church

However, the Church's blindness is not entirely due to lack of revelation. For some, it can be the result of "church anti-Semitism." For others it is an inability to deal with the guilt many Christians feel toward the Jewish nation because of the Holocaust.

Many Gentile believers have a deep sense of regret for the Church's tragic relationship to Israel. Thorough repentance and cleansing from all anti-Semitism (as is happening today among many Christians from all nations and denominations) is God's path out of all past guilt.

The restoration of Israel

This allows for an entirely new beginning where one can delve into God's true purposes for Israel in the light of his revelation, with a pure heart of love and dedication. God is calling the true bridal Church into the fullness of his end-time purposes, in order to receive his heart, to pay the price and to pray for the spiritual rebirth of Israel.

We know that the "dry bones" of the Jewish people have come together and the national rebirth of Israel in the Promised Land has taken place (Ezekiel 37). But just as the prophet Ezekiel said, Israel is still spiritually dead because it has not yet received the life-bringing breath of God.

God is truly working in the land of Israel in many wonderful ways, but the nation is still separated from its God by a great gulf. The "remnant" of Jews and Gentiles who have been born of the Spirit and who live in unity in the land are beginning to bridge this gap. Spiritual restoration has begun.

This work of restoration is twofold:

1. The salvation of the remainder of Israel.
2. The rebuilding of his spiritual house through the revelation of the "new person" in Christ – Jewish and Gentile hearts united in the Messiah.

Blindness toward Jesus

Unfortunately, the Talmud (Jewish commentary on the Old Testament Scriptures) has replaced Israel's new covenant inheritance with a substitute religious system which has no life or salvation. The Talmudic veil, coupled with Jewish persecution by the Church and false Christian theology, have deepened the root of unbelief in the Jewish heart and increased their blindness toward Jesus.

Judaism today

Judaism today is only a shadow of the old covenant faith. It has become a highly developed humanistic and legalistic system which takes pride in its religious achievements and wisdom. Orthodox Judaism still retains elements of genuine belief and the fear of God, but it cannot offer salvation or transformation of the heart. It has often alienated Jewish people from their God.

Many Israelis have confused rabbinical Judaism with the God of Israel and therefore want nothing to do with him. Others, because that is all they know, attempt to serve God through Judaism (the rabbinic system) and strive to be faithful to him within this system.

Some have seen the difference between the biblical inheritance and this religious system and are groping their way toward the living God of the Bible. They sense deep inside that the glory of his *shekinah* – his presence among his people – departed long ago.

Jesus is the key

Of course, Jesus is the key to understanding this dilemma. He is the only way to find the God of Israel and our true biblical inheritance.

The historic and prophetic destiny of Israel is closely connected to this revelation of the Messiah. What God is doing with Israel as a nation in the Promised Land serves to fulfill his promise that Jesus will in the end be revealed to his people. There is no other way to understand this.

No relationship to God

Judaism is bankrupt because it cannot offer salvation, redemption or eternal life, let alone a relationship with the living God.

> *"For the Israelites will live many days without king or prince, without sacrifice or sacred stones, without ephod or idol. Afterward the Israelites will return and seek the LORD their God and David their king. They will come trembling to the LORD and to his blessings in the last days."*
>
> (Hosea 3:4–5)

It is painful to be aware of the Jewish people's present situation. Israel's lack of relationship with God makes it even more clear how urgent it is to bring the good news back to this people. These are the people, after all, to whom it was first of all offered and promised.

Jews find the Messiah Jesus

Since the reunification of Jerusalem in 1967 (as prophesied in Luke 21:24, *"Jerusalem will be trampled on by the Gentiles until the times of the Gentiles are fulfilled"*), more Jews have been finding the Messiah. Jesus has revealed himself to many of them through a clear and direct encounter. But most have come to know him through others who have shared the Gospel and their personal testimonies.

Today God is working in Israel in various ways to bring the Gospel back to the Jewish people. It is clearly the prophetic hour in God's timetable for Israel, but this has also been brought about by the worldwide Church's increasing intercession on behalf of Israel.

Both Jewish and Gentile believers who are serving God in Israel are bringing the Gospel to the Jewish people. Many Gentile Christians are serving sacrificially in deep love and humility to bring about the salvation of Israel.

God courts his people

There is now greater openness to the Gospel than ever, but a much stronger hunger for God is still needed. The extremely difficult situation in the land is part of God's way of drawing his people to himself and preparing them for the harvest. The unlimited salvation and revival which we see in Zechariah 12 will come through the outpouring of the Holy Spirit.

The Church's calling

The Lord wants to give his burden of prayer for Israel to many more persons in the Church. The Church is called to seek him in fasting and prayer, in weeping and travail, for the fulfillment of God's ultimate redemptive purpose for Israel. This event will flow over into the end-time, worldwide salvation and the revelation of God to all humanity.

9 781852 407308